The HR Guide to European Mergers and Acquisitions

T0371888

*To my mother and father
who gave me the inspiration and determination
to write this book.*

*To my wife Dany,
with whom I successfully merged 20 years ago,
and to our children,
Jenny
and
Anthony*

The HR Guide to European Mergers and Acquisitions

James F. Klein

with Robert-Charles Kahn

Routledge
Taylor & Francis Group

LONDON AND NEW YORK

First published 2003 by Gower Publishing

Published 2016 by Routledge
2 Park Square, Milton Park, Abingdon, Oxfordshire OX14 4RN
711 Third Avenue, New York, NY 10017, USA

First issued in paperback 2016

Routledge is an imprint of the Taylor & Francis Group, an informa business

British Library Cataloguing in Publication Data

Klein, James F.
    The HR guide to European mergers and acquisitions
    1. Consolidation and merger of corporations - Europe
    2. Personnel management - Europe
    I. Title II. Kahn, Robert-Charles
    658.1'6

Library of Congress Cataloging-in-Publication Data

Klein, James F., 1957-
    The HR guide to European mergers and acquisitions / James F. Klein with Robert-Charles Kahn.
        p. cm.
    ISBN 0-566-08564-X
    1. Consolidation and merger of corporations--Europe--Management. 2. Consolidation and merger of corporations--Psychological aspects--Europe. 3. Personnel management--Europe. I. Kahn, Robert-Charles, 1963- II. Title.

    HD2746.55.E8K54 2003
    658.3--dc21
                                                                        2003044835

ISBN 13: 978-1-138-26916-3 (pbk)
ISBN 13: 978-0-566-08564-2 (hbk)

Contents

Part II: The transition period

Part III: The integration stage

Appendices

List of tables and figures

PART III

Tables

Figures

Acknowledgements

When I started writing this book, I received support from numerous friends, colleagues and business partners who, through anecdotes, documents or general advice helped me structure, document and complete my manuscript.

There are, however, two people to whom I would particularly like to express my gratitude: Robert-Charles Kahn, my co-author, who contributed substantially to the overall structure of the book and, in particular, to the topic of communication, and Peter Rupf, Director of Operations with Lenz Staehlin, Geneva, whose outstanding analytical and critical mind, insightful comments and contributions, and unwavering enthusiasm throughout my project, proved an invaluable contribution to this book's contents.

Foreword

The human factor is one of the most decisive elements to make or break merger and acquisition (M&A) work. Time and time again, seasoned professionals agree that once a deal is completed the real work begins. From my own experience it is this work that is vital to graft two entities together, to make them tick as one, and it is a task whose difficulties are only increased through the cross-border deals.

If you are planning any M&A work, James Klein's book is an essential read – it is dedicated to the linkage between the deal itself and the end result. There is not much available on the bookshelves that is as 'hands on' or as user friendly as this volume. But after reading it, I don't believe you will need any other. It is the blueprint to successful implementation and completion of M&A work.

The author is right in dissecting this seemingly huge task, rendering it tangible. He breaks down the major components into concrete steps thereby enabling the reader to actually drive through the integration using a detailed and comprehensive roadmap. The book succeeds because it is a practical, hands-on guide rather than a general and theoretical essay, and because it provides the reader with the steps, tools, sequence of events and material to successfully complete the human resources integration following a merger.

Beyond the purely technical aspects, the author includes comparative tables, tips and stories illustrating the differences, specificities and pitfalls particular to the different European countries. Klein's vision of M&A integration captures the essence of the hard and soft techniques needed to drive the integration process. His attention to the major human resource issues makes for not only a good business book, but also one the reader will want to begin to use immediately.

The book is primarily addressed to an audience that is planning, or in the midst of, M&A activities in Europe. However, I believe that readers throughout the world, not just from Europe, will benefit from the approach.

Mihir K. Som, Vice Chairman and General Manager, Lockheed Martin International SA, Geneva, Switzerland

Vice President Finance and Administration, Continental Europe, Africa and Middle East, Lockheed Martin Global Inc., Bethesda, USA

Preface

Many books and studies have been published on the unsatisfactory outcome of most mergers and acquisitions, which generally result in unrealized synergies and improvements for the acquiring company's financial performance, an overall deterioration of competitive positioning, and in particular, the loss of key human resources.

The reasons for these disappointments are numerous but can be summarized into two main factors: first, the candour with which many CEOs and 'deal-makers' chronically overestimate the cooperation and support they will receive in the integration process from the management of *both* companies involved; and secondly, the degree to which they then underestimate – or simply overlook – the costs of such an integration.

In her book *When Giants Learn To Dance*,[1] Rosabeth Moss Kanter illustrates how confusion, misinformation, emotional leakage, breakdown of energy and weakened faith in a leader's ability to deliver, are amongst the key threats to an integration process.

The HR Guide to European Mergers and Acquisitions is based on over 20 years of experience in human resources, and on a number of small to medium-size pan-European mergers and acquisitions. It will give you the means to minimize the threats to successful completion of M&A integrations, and will provide you with a step-by-step process on how to prepare, conduct, implement and communicate the integration of human resources in a newly combined organization.

This book will also provide you with a structured approach, including sample processes, charts, forms and checklists, to help you put together an overall human resources plan, and manage it to successful completion. It includes a number of do's and don'ts, illustrated by some case stories from my experience and which I trust you will find useful when confronted with alternative paths to follow.

While the principles illustrated here apply to M&A in general, emphasis has been put on the European approach to integration processes and this work is based on the 'European' perspective.

1 Moss Kanter, Rosabeth (1990) *When Giants Learn To Dance*, A Touchstone Book published by Simon & Schuster Inc. New York.

Introduction

The significant problems we face cannot be solved at the same level of thinking we were at when we created them.

Albert Einstein (1879–1955)

News of an acquisition[1] is an event in the life of a company, which inevitably stirs uncertainty, anxiety, and often loss of motivation amongst the personnel of both companies involved.

There is no magical formula to avoid these side effects totally; however there are tools to significantly reduce them and to mitigate their effects. Whether you are the Integration Manager, Human Resources Director or CEO of either one of the companies involved, the faith people will have in your ability to bring the acquisition to a successful and rewarding completion will be governed by the trust employees have in you. This faith will be based upon:

1. *An in-depth understanding of each company.* You need to take the time to master the differences and similarities of each company's products, clients, marketing tools, objectives, processes, challenges and, of course, corporate identity. It is one of the key tools without which gaining credibility; attention and respect from the employees of the acquired company will be a difficult undertaking.

2. *Empowerment and ownership of the process.* Both are key issues, all too often underestimated. Responsibility for integration must be clearly defined and not moved from one executive or consultant to another. Integration managers must have the authority for decision-making within a clear scope of their assignments, and integration streams must have stable and coherent reporting lines.

    Of course, an integration process must remain a flexible one. Throughout the course of the process, priorities may change, people may leave, and

---

1 In order to facilitate the reading of this book, the word *acquisition* will refer equally to mergers and acquisitions, which is also abreviated at times as M&A's.

strategies may be re-adapted to circumstances. Nevertheless, the first reassuring signs of stability and continuity that you can provide are an empowered leader, an established process and a set time-frame to achieve defined objectives.

3. ***Speed of action and decisiveness***. This is another area where, as integration manager, your ability to address issues quickly and efficiently, which may have been overlooked or deliberately ignored during the pre-acquisition phase, will be constantly challenged. These issues may vary from the accounting or reporting systems used in each company to compensation of the sales force, client billing procedures, potential cannibalisation of products, and so on.

   Although you need transition periods to assess the advantages and disadvantages of such conflicting systems more effectively – particularly in the areas of employees' compensation and general terms of employment – I have found it often preferable to impose a clear direction quickly (generally that of the acquiring company) and then build on it, rather than to spend months in costly assessments. Indeed, assessments do not invariably lead to the right decisions and in the worst-case scenario, they can take so long to complete that you run the risk of **needing to make up your mind before the assessment is completed.** When this happens – and it happens more often than not – it will seriously undermine the credibility of the decision, the assessment process and the leader who recommended it.

4. ***Communication style***. This, of course, is one of the most important issues in the integration process. Failure to communicate will inevitably lead to rumours, misinformation, unfounded fears and ultimately a poisoned working atmosphere, which will not only strain the process, but can also jeopardise its very completion.

I have mentioned the importance of empowerment. This applies particularly to communication. If your company does not have an internal PR or Communications Manager, I can only urge you to hire an outside communications consultant *on an in-house basis*.

In the following chapters, I will lead you step-by-step through the different stages of the HR integration process. Each of these steps will be covered by an individual chapter and will provide you with procedures, sample charts, checklists and pointers.

The complete process includes:

1. Integration planning:
   - Understanding the deal
   - Due Diligence process
   - Integration teams
   - Emergency retention programmes
   - Communication plan.

2. Building the grounds for a common HR policy:
   • Comparison of terms of employment
   • Analysis of compensation and benefits
   • Definition of data transfer (HRMIS)[2] needs
   • Assessment of corporate handbooks and procedures
   • Securing key employees.

3. The integration process:
   • Review of processes and functional terminology
   • Establish manpower planning and requirement checks
   • Conduct organization and assessment programmes
   • Appreciate local labour law
   • Prepare and conduct terminations
   • Finalize transfers and the overall integration.

This process is illustrated in the summary diagram overleaf.

2 Human Resources Information Systems.

THE TRANSITION AND INTEGRATION PROCESS

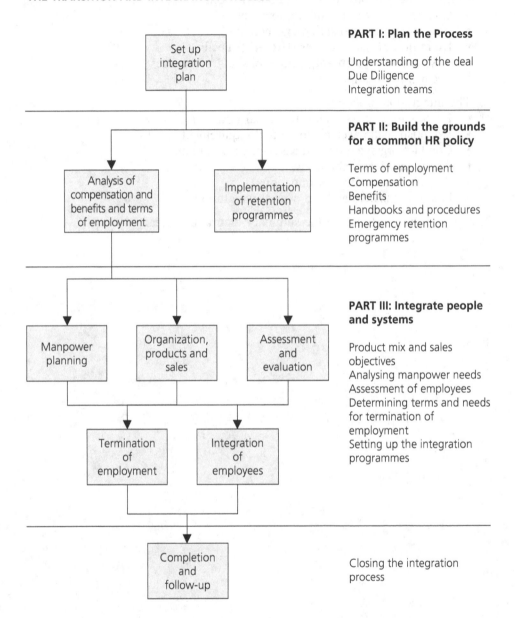

PART I: Plan the Process

Understanding of the deal
Due Diligence
Integration teams

PART II: Build the grounds for a common HR policy

Terms of employment
Compensation
Benefits
Handbooks and procedures
Emergency retention programmes

PART III: Integrate people and systems

Product mix and sales objectives
Analysing manpower needs
Assessment of employees
Determining terms and needs for termination of employment
Setting up the integration programmes

Closing the integration process

The flowchart boxes read:

- Set up integration plan
- Analysis of compensation and benefits and terms of employment
- Implementation of retention programmes
- Manpower planning
- Organization, products and sales
- Assessment and evaluation
- Termination of employment
- Integration of employees
- Completion and follow-up

Part I

The early stages

You got to be careful if you don't know where you're going, because you might not get there.

Yogi Berra

This section will cover:

- Necessary questions for a good general understanding of the deal
- Essential points of a Due Diligence report
- Key steps in an integration plan
- Main components of a communication plan

Chapter 1

Understanding the objectives, scope and expectations following a merger

You need to gain a good understanding of both companies if you are to focus on the right priorities from the very beginning of the process. This is not only a question of understanding products, clients and market share, but also of obtaining an accurate feeling for corporate values, working styles, and methods. By taking the time to ask questions, you will gain early insight of where people see the strengths and weaknesses of the deal, how they perceive they might win or lose in the process, and which parts of the process will require more attention, diplomacy or *savoir faire*.

Even if you were not involved in the pre-merger discussions and only brought in to handle the Human Resources integration after the deal was signed, it is unlikely that the final organization chart, reporting lines and functional responsibilities will have been fully defined. Therefore, you will need to gain a thorough understanding of both companies' approach to business to provide valuable and reliable input throughout the integration process.

Getting information

If you have not been involved in the early stages of the deal, your first step will be to obtain this information quickly.

The CEO, CFO and COO will be the obvious first people to go to, if they can find the time to sit down with you and go through the rationale of the deal.

If you are a public listed company, an Offer to Shareholders will invariably have been prepared, which will provide you with information on:

- The background and reasons for the offer
- A summary of each company including:
  - operations, objectives and strategy
  - services and products
  - cooperation and alliances
  - group structure and personnel
- The financial reports.

All of which will help you in getting a preliminary overview.

The next step is to compile all of this information and prepare the communication plan. Make sure that you rely solely on information coming from authorized personnel. Answering questions from troubled co-workers with statements such as 'I believe, I have heard ... it is possible ...' will not help you gain time but, on the contrary, only add to confusion.

If you don't have the answer to a question, just say so, make it a point to enquire about it, and when you have the answer, communicate it. The questions in Checklist 1 are a useful starting point for your communication plan.

Checklist 1: Getting the complete picture

- What are the key objectives of the deal? *For example: Eliminating a competitor, gaining market share, gaining technical expertise, growing the balance sheet, attracting key executives, broadening the scope of products, gaining international exposure, etc.*
- What are the timing and milestones to close the deal?
- Is there a preliminary vision of what the new organization chart will look like?
- How will product lines, sales areas, customer care be affected?
- How will the deal affect the headcount?
- What level of confidentiality is needed when addressing the above?
- Are there key employees to the deal who must be retained?
- Has a legal network been set-up to deal with local legal issues? Who can have direct access to it?
- Are there any countries or districts that require special attention or handling and why?
- What systems, procedures, accounting/reporting principles will be given priority?
- Have transitional decisions already been taken regarding functional reporting, compensation and commissions of sales staff, performance measurements, product lines, overlapping products, functions or countries, etc.?
- Have integration group leaders already been identified to handle the above?
- Who is handling the communication of the acquisition, both externally and internally, and what is the core message?
- Is the acquired company, or any of its subsidiaries or branches unionized? How have the unions reacted to the deal?
- If the acquisition includes international branches or subsidiaries, how will the local boards be reshuffled?
- Likewise, who will act as country Managing Director *ad interim*? And how and when will this be communicated?
- How does the deal affect employee stock option ownership?

- Are there any objections or reservations to the deal that have been voiced by members of one or the other company's top management?
- Has an Integration Manager been appointed in the acquired company? Have his or her reporting and cooperation guidelines been clearly established?

Chapter 2

HR Due Diligence

What is a Due Diligence report?

Due Diligence is a form of risk management most commonly known as '*doing your homework before you invest*'. The sample checklist below[1] is an example of the issues, which are examined, in the pre-acquisition phase. As this book focuses primarily on HR integration, Checklist 2 largely ignores non-HR topics.

Checklist 2: Sample Due Diligence items

- **Corporate Organization**
  - Articles of Incorporation
  - Corporate structure
  - Shareholder list, and agreements
- **Financial Information**
  - Annual and quarterly financial information over the past three to five years
  - Financial projections
  - Capital structure
- **Products**
  - Product offering
  - Description of products
  - Major contracts by product line
- **Customer Information**
  - List of top 10 to 15 customers
  - List of strategic relationships
  - List of 10 to 15 suppliers

---

1 *Deloitte & Touche: Growth Company Services Due Diligence Check List (with slight amendments brought by author).*

- **Competition**
  - Description of competitive landscape
  - Trade publications
- **Sales and Marketing**
  - Strategy and implementation
  - Sales productivity models and pricing strategy
  - Distribution channels
- **Management and Personnel**
  - Organization chart and summary biographies of top management
  - Historical and projected headcount by function and location
  - Compensation and contractual terms of employment
  - Pension plans and medical benefits
  - Employee relations
- **Legal and Administrative Matters**
  - Pending lawsuits
  - Safety and environment issues and liabilities
  - Patents, copyrights, licences, etc.

I believe that the Human Resources Director should be brought in early rather than late in an M&A project. However, I have experienced a number of acquisitions where the Chief Finance Officer or M&A Director has conducted Due Diligence reviews that include key HR issues, without the involvement of the Human Resources Director. The HR Director was simply brought in at a later stage to validate or complete the findings and voice any additional concerns considered important.

Besides the unnecessary duplication of tasks this approach will create, it often leaves the door open to unexpected issues which should have been considered in the preliminary survey, particularly in relationship to direct and indirect financial implications associated with varying corporate policies and commitments, international labour legislation and unions.

To illustrate this, think about how your company records costs for personnel on temporary or consulting assignments. Although many European accounting legislations impose a predetermined accounting format for such issues, others do not and in such instances, these costs may not be included in personnel and temporary headcount, but integrated, for example, in 'operational costs and services', thus giving a misleading representation of manpower needs and costs.

In any event, an in-depth HR Due Diligence review should be carried out before the final deal is completed. It should further represent one of the cornerstones in the preparation of a merger integration plan.[2]

---

2 A merger integration plan defines how assets, products, Human Resources and processes will be combined in the new organization. Prepared in written form, the post-merger integration plan not only outlines how this approach will enable the merged companies to achieve their strategic goals, but also provides some key answers to the reasons why the acquisition was done in the first place.

Key components of an HR Due Diligence report

When conducting an HR Due Diligence review, you will be looking for facts, which may have:

- Direct financial implications (hard facts)
- Indirect financial implications (soft facts)
- Miscellaneous implications.

Hard facts are generally fairly easy to collect and analyse as they are based on written documents such as working contracts, payroll records, standard agreements as well as statistical and analytical data.

But many other 'intangible' facts will come out as you talk with people. To get the information about these intangibles requires the ability to create trust and confidence between yourself and the people you will be interviewing.

One mistake that some integration group leaders make when conducting a Due Diligence process is to adopt a hard-line investigator attitude. They focus essentially on collecting hard facts, on inquiring on the why's and how's of findings without attempting to understand the history of them, and on inquisitively searching for wrongful practices.

An acquisition invariably generates high emotional strain, particularly on the employees of the acquired company. Establishing a relationship of trust between yourself (or the integration manager) and the people in the departments you are reviewing implies taking a lot of time talking with those people, whatever their level or role in the organizations. It is amazing how much valuable information support staff and secretaries hold on management styles, corporate values, and general working atmosphere.

Building trust implies handling the other team as if you actually were their manager, looking after and caring for them, listening to their worries and concerns, coaching them through the process and offering a reassuring note where and when needed. By applying this approach, you should succeed in overcoming, or considerably reducing employees' resistance to cooperate – an unfortunate but natural human reaction when faced with fear or uncertainty – and a reaction often characteristic of a Due Diligence process.

Facts with direct financial implications (hard facts)

Facts with direct financial implications can be split into two categories:

1. Present financial commitments.
2. Future financial commitments.

The merger integration plan should be distributed early to the company's top management and later to all staff (probably in summarized form). As for all documents of this nature, a legal counsel should review it prior to distribution.

Present financial commitments relate primarily to compensation, corporate benefits, pension fund funding, medical coverage, etc. whereas future financial commitments will focus on special agreements, bonus schemes, stock-option agreements, golden parachutes, training commitments, non-competition clauses, etc.

When conducting the Due Diligence investigation, keep in mind that you are not only gathering data which will help you compare practices, policies and benefits between the two companies, *but also identify underlying financial commitments which may become a concern at a later stage.* Amongst the foremost of these, I suggest you pay special attention to:

Non-competition clauses. In many European countries (and particularly in Germany, Denmark, Finland and Norway) non-competition clauses imply financial commitments which can have serious impact in the post-acquisition integration costs. Heavy indemnities will need to be paid out to employees who have them, whether they are terminated by their company, or resign of their own free will. Besides, attempting to waive the non-competition clause will not waive the financial penalties set forth in the contract unless agreed *by both parties.* It is therefore extremely important that you get all possible information on the existence of such clauses in each country. You may discover that in some countries, non-competition clauses are regularly used, whereas in others they are not. And these variations in policy may come from constraint in local labour law or simply from the local General Manager's approach to non-competition clauses.

It may also be the case that such clauses are not in the employment contract itself, but are part of a collective agreement, which can be at corporate or local level.

Termination agreements. For management positions, it has become general practice in Europe to include in the employment contract, the financial terms which will govern non-voluntary termination of employment for causes other than the employee's incompetence (restructuring, economic grounds, M&A's, transfer of operations, etc.).

Although the European Union is attempting to standardize employment, termination policies and practices throughout its member states, only a few directives of this nature have been enforced as laws. As a result, particular attention needs to be given, country by country, not only to the contractual clauses governing an employee's termination, but also to their full compliance with the labour laws of the country where the employee is based. This is particularly true when examining the contracts of expatriate staff. In Part III, Chapter 4, I have presented a series of comparative tables showing the minimum legal requirements governing termination of employment in a number of EU states.

Stock options. There are as many stock option regulations in Europe as there are individual countries. I have often encountered situations where it was taken for granted that the rules and regulations governing a corporate stock option programme was 'universal'. And this belief invariably leads to major problems. For example, in some countries, local law stipulates that stock options are immediately vested and exercisable at the time of a merger or acquisition (regardless of what the stock option contract may say). In others, there is no such law.

Some countries will impose a minimum or maximum vesting period for the plan to benefit from tax and social deduction advantages. Here, again, this is not a standard European practice. Other countries will require that no more than a certain percentage may exist between the offering price and an average market price at the time of issue.

Finally, in some countries, you can be taxed on 'theoretical' capital gain – that is to say the difference between the offer and the market value – even before the beneficiary exercises his options.

When tax-effective compensation becomes ineffective

One of the companies I worked for had established a stock option plan that stated in writing that:

Profits employees would achieve through the plan would be taxed according to local laws on stock options benefit plans, and in case of a merger or acquisition, only vested options could be exercised.

Of the problems they ran into shortly after launching the plan and which reached a climax when they were acquired a few months later, one is particularly relevant to an HR Due Diligence report.

The original stock option rules and regulations had been drafted by the US head office and introduced into the European subsidiaries on the assumption that by providing a clause stipulating that the plan would be taxed *according to local laws on stock options*, any specific issues that might arise would therefore adjust automatically.

In France, particularly, this assumption had devastating effects: indeed, the plan included a number of articles which contravened French law on stock options, the foremost of which were the duration of the vesting period imposed and the purchase price offered which both contravened the French legal dispositions on stock option plans.

Furthermore, the selling company having wrongly considered that employees with non-vested stock options had no right to exercise them following the acquisition (as stipulated in the original plan), was consequently faced with the fact that they had *de facto* presented an incorrect stock ownership report to the purchasing party. In order to straighten things out in a speedy and timely manner, and not be faced with the embarrassment of having presented a wrong stock ownership report, the acquired company asked the employees concerned to waive their stock option rights against an equal compensation in cash, specifying in writing that the cash compensation would be treated with the full tax-effective benefits of a regular stock option programme.

Unfortunately, and because of the articles contravening French law, the plan was not considered by the French authorities as a stock option plan but as a deferred compensation system and consequently fully taxable and fully subject to social security deductions. As a result, the impact on the company's liabilities for social security contributions was suddenly well over the analysis presented in the Due Diligence review.

And finally, having committed to a tax-effective payment of the shares, the acquired company had to proceed with a gross-up of the payments made so that the net in-pocket return of the transaction would equal the amount that employees would have normally received, had they exercised their options within a normal procedure.

Do not, therefore, take it for granted that because a corporate lawyer has drafted the stock option plan, and because it is bullet-proof in the country of issue, it necessarily complies with all European legislation.

Other considerations, such as Pension Fund funding, medical coverage, training commitments, etc. also need to be looked into with detail, not only because of their financial implications, but because they will need careful consideration when defining the new organization's corporate benefit policies, which, if less generous than the previous company's, may have considerable impact on employee morale and motivation.

Finally, ensure that compliance checks have been carried out carefully, and that there are no labour laws which are not, or only partially, respected. In particular that:

* Social security and insurance charges are fully paid up
* Safety measures and regulations are respected
* Working hours and overtime do not exceed the legal maximum
* Employee representation (unions) comply with statutory dispositions.

Facts with indirect financial implications (soft facts)

One of the most interesting parts of an HR Due Diligence review, in my view, is to 'take the pulse' of HR within an organization, measuring its heartbeat through indicators such as employee turnover, absenteeism, length and quantity of job vacancies, etc.

Succession needs (short and long term) – including the risk of losing key players as a result of the acquisition – are also part of this review and should be carefully looked at.

High turnover may be trade-specific, and in many circumstances not a truly revealing factor of employee dissatisfaction or mismanagement. It should nevertheless be flagged and investigated with care, as costs of new hires (agencies, head-hunters, etc.), introductory training and induction programmes, as well as management time can quickly and considerably overburden an HR budget.

Absenteeism[3] is a very interesting indicator of employee dissatisfaction and management inadequacies. It rarely hits the whole organization but is generally endemic in single units, departments or even single plants. If absence records are well kept, it is easy to single out the recurrence of those '*Monday morning headaches*' and '*Wednesday afternoon stomach cramps*' which, as common as they may appear at first sight, are warning signals that something isn't quite right and will require your closer attention.

Finally, *succession* – whether because of retirement, transfers, or replacements – also has indirect financial implications, which you will want to examine. This should include assessing the risk of losing key people to the organization because of the acquisition, and examining how to reduce that risk by implementing a retention programme, for example. This will be examined more closely in Part II, Chapter 5.

Facts with miscellaneous implications

A good HR Due Diligence review does not limit itself to hard and soft facts but also requires a certain amount of intuition and pre-analysis, as well as good understanding of local laws and mindsets.

What I include in facts with miscellaneous implications are events, situations – even perceptions – that could tarnish the company's global image or reputation and potentially represent financial liabilities.

If the acquired company has conducted employee surveys, be sure to obtain copies and analyse them as they often represent a good indicator of employee sources of satisfaction and concern. Most surveys also include a section on management and leadership and how their peers perceive the company's leaders.

Any history of HR-related lawsuits is another area that deserves special attention. It is not so much the quantity of the complaints, nor how many have been won or lost in the past couple of years that should be of most concern to you, but more the pattern of complaints (and whether they are restricted to some departments in particular) which should deserve your careful attention.

In most European countries, where protection of employment is a key component to labour relations, HR cases brought before labour courts are more often than not related to disputes on unfair dismissals or general terms governing termination of employment. As a result (and without in any way minimizing the importance of understanding the story behind such cases), complaints for unsafe working conditions, bullying, sexual harassment, discrimination or any other forms of unlawful behaviour should trigger your immediate concern and further investigation.

---

3 There is a clear difference between absenteeism and sick leave. Absenteeism is characterized by a short-term absence (generally ranging from an afternoon to two days) decided by the employees themselves for minor ailments such as headaches, cramps, flu, etc...., whereas sick leave is a medically ordered absence from work of greater than three to four days.

Finally, you will want to know if the acquired company has faced industrial action from trade unions, what the reasons were, and how management handled the situation. If the company is unionized or has a workers' council or representative body, it is important to get a good understanding of the degree of confidence which exists between management and employee representatives, and the key areas of concern and expectations.

All of the above will give you invaluable information on corporate image, management style and overall employee satisfaction of the acquired company, and will provide you with the first areas of focus when proceeding with the integration of the workforce itself.

Summary

An HR Due Diligence review is designed to inform the acquiring company of all problems, liabilities, trends and other factors related to Human Resources that may affect the acquiring company's ability to reach the goals and objectives of the acquisition. It is an essential part of the global Due Diligence process, and includes a review of all the legal, financial, operational, commercial and strategic elements in the acquired company's operating history, contractual relationships and organizational structure.

This review is critical. The implications it may have can directly impact on the financial analysis of the deal itself and consequently on its validity or valuation. It will also be a key tool to ensuring the smooth integration of the workforce itself after the deal has been completed.

A standard HR Due Diligence review collects facts and figures and analyses them through an objective lens. But don't forget that a *good* HR Due Diligence review takes human factors into account too.

An in-depth, thorough and complete HR Due Diligence review will spotlight the hard facts. If you also take into account the emotions, worries, and concerns of those you have spoken to, when compiling the information, these will reveal the shadows – which may either harden or soften the general picture – but without which your global assessment will remain a purely 'mathematical' representation of the situation. See Table 1.

Table 1 *HR Due Diligence checklist*

	Compared with acquiring company	Potential liabilities	
		Compliance checked	Potential costs involved
General compensation items			
Salaries of management			
Salaries of employees			
Commission systems			
Profit participation schemes			
Bonus and financial commitments			
Contractual termination agreement			
Non-competition clauses			
Special retirement plans			
Stock option plans			
Tax effective compensation systems			
Benefits			
Holidays			
Sick/Maternity leave			
Sabbatical leaves			
Training commitments			
Pension plan			
Health/Accident insurance			
Life insurance			
Company cars			
Lunch facilities			
Clubs and entertainment			
Other benefits			
HR systems			
HR MIS systems and compatibility			
Cost of maintenance			
Accuracy and availability of data			
Manpower needed for maintenance			
Statistical data			
Turnover			
Absenteeism			
On/Off site accidents			
Overtime			
Women in management			
Age groups (and pre-retirement issues)			
Educational level			

Chapter 3
Setting up an integration plan

What is an integration plan?

The integration plan is a tool to monitor and manage the different steps that need to be addressed during the integration process. It is designed to schedule actions and set deadlines, allocate responsibilities, monitor progress, provide feedback, and ensure the adaptability to change in the integration process.

What you first need to establish is:

- Who owns the plan?
- Who manages and coaches the plan owner?
- What project management tools should be used?
- How to establish your integration plan
- Emergency measures.

In a number of M&A integration guides, you may find that defining the integration plan comes in as the first step in the process and not as a second step after the Due Diligence review.

How and what to prioritize is very much a personal matter, and the order presented in this book is by no means a rigid recommendation. As you review your priorities and objectives, you may of course choose a different sequence according to your own working style.

There are two reasons why I have chosen the process described in this chapter. First, the Due Diligence review is a pre-acquisition process whereas the integration plan comes into force once the deal has been signed. As a result, you will probably find it easier to set your priorities in correct order and select the right integration team once you have identified the key issues. This strategy will also avoid the need to redesign parts of the plan and reorganize teams just after the completion of the Due Diligence review and identification of areas of priority. As mentioned earlier, consistency in your approach is vital to maintain credibility and motivation.

Second, there is the question of speed to consider. During the pre-acquisition period, time may be too short to go into all the details of compensation, benefits and HR procedures. As a result, the HR Due Diligence review will focus on identifying main areas of potential concern or liability, whereas the integration plan will need to go into the specific details to ensure a smooth transition.

Who owns the plan?

To the question 'Should someone be designated chief planner for the integration?', some authors on M&A integration say 'no', arguing that the best post-merger plans are ultimately created by groups.[1]

Although there is no question that you will need to create teams, and that specific groups of people should address specific groups of questions, I believe that an integration plan without a chief planner would have a lot in common with a symphony orchestra without a conductor.

Choosing the right chief planner is a delicate matter and a vital component of the process's success. The hierarchical levels of the individuals, their main area of business, whether they are an outside consultant or come from the acquiring or acquired company, are not critical. Key considerations include the individual's:

- Autonomy and empowerment
- Leadership skills and ability to delegate
- Planning skills
- Communication skills
- Empathy and charisma.

In the Introduction, I stressed the importance of empowerment. Although the ultimate decisions on key implementation processes will probably revert to the CEO, the chief planner (or integration manager) must have the authority to decide on the choice of processes, courses of actions, staffing of the integration teams, and disclosure and timing of communication.

Put simply, the CEO or M&A Director should designate and clearly empower one individual to set up, manage and coach the global integration process.

Who manages and coaches the integration plan owner?

This question often depends on the size or geography of the company. As a full integration process includes merging finance, general operations and sales, as well as Human Resources, the chief operating and chief financial officers or even the M&A Director may retain responsibility for the integration itself. In most cases however, the integration manager will report to the CEO.

It is most important to ensure that one person, and one person alone, manages the integration plan owner and does not interfere with the groups that he or she will subsequently set up.

1 Alexandra Reed Lajoux (1998) *The Art of M&A Integration*, McGraw-Hill.

What project management tools should be used?

The choice of the project management software will again depend largely on the size of the acquisition, the sophistication of the resource allocation, and the type and amount of documentation or information which you want to include in the plan.

If you are leading a straightforward process, with dedicated resources and support allotted to you, a simple spreadsheet will probably prove sufficient. However, if your project requires time management or shuffling of resources, because members of your group can only devote a limited amount of time per day or week to the process, monitor integration costs; or if you need to handle a very complex process with scheduled interdependencies, you may find it useful to use one of the project management tools such as Microsoft Project®.

How to establish your integration plan

It is important that you set aside time to formulate the different stages of the plan you will be managing, before you actually start. An integration plan is an evolving process which can get easily out of hand if you do not establish very early on what needs to be accomplished (in priority), what interdependencies exist between the processes, and how to handle the unexpected without losing track of your plan.

You will need to define strict deadlines for each individual handling part of the project. Make sure you adhere strictly to your own deadlines and when doing so, assess the consequences of late delivery on such items. This will also help you plan for contingencies.

The following sample project plan is based on the earlier HR Due Diligence review which has been broken down into further detail. The detail will be examined more closely in Part II in the form of project sheets designed to help analyse the differences both between the two companies, and samples of European national labour and social laws.

Please note that although the plan shown in Table 2 includes topics which are not strictly HR, such as communication, products and sales, its main focus remains the integration of Human Resources.

Setting up the plan

Assign responsibilities and empower leaders

Once your integration plan is established, you will need to set up a team to carry out the various actions you have identified. Since we are looking at the integration of European companies, bear in mind that we are reviewing several countries, managed by country directors and reporting to their respective headquarters. You will also need to scale up your plan appropriately unless the acquired company is

Table 2   Integration plan

Item	Action	Responsible manager	To be actioned by	Deadline	Progress report
Steps to the integration plan	1. Setting up the plan 2. Prepare the communication plan 3. Compare terms of employment 4. Compare benefits 5. Compare systems and policies 6. Emergency measures: Prepare retention programmes 7. Review global processes 8. Conduct manpower planning, assessments and redundancies 9. Finalize transfers and integration				
1. Setting up the plan	Assign responsibilities and empower leaders Define integration team organization Define the basis and timelines for reporting				
2. Prepare the communication plan	Empower the communication team leader Agree HR communication milestones and key stakeholders Define communication tools Develop questions and answers and communication guidelines				
3. Compare terms of employment	Analyse differences in contractual terms of employment Review the employment contracts Analyse salary and commission systems				
4. Compare benefits	Compare medical coverage Compare old age and retirement benefits Compare life insurances Social and other benefits				
5. Compare systems and policies	HRMIS systems, tools and date transfer Compare general policies and handbooks				
6. Prepare retention programmes	Programmes to retain key players during the integration process Programmes to retain employees throughout the process				
7. Review global processes	Review products and sales Review vocabulary used for job description and responsibilities				
8. Conduct manpower planning, assessments and redundancies	Define manpower needs Conduct assessments and skill reviews Define redundancy strategy and guidelines Establish termination and severance package guidelines Implement helpdesks and hotlines				
9. Finalize transfers and integration	Announce transfers, appointments and new reporting lines Integrate new employees Provide coaching, follow up and feedback				

well structured and process oriented. Draw up a matrix of reporting responsibilities to ensure everyone can see and understand the various roles within the integration team.

An integration chart might look like something like Figure 1.

The next step will be selecting your team leaders. Here too, you will be looking for similar qualities and abilities to those mentioned earlier for the integration manager.

Your team leaders – as well as other members of specific groups – should be made up of employees of both the acquiring and acquired company. It is vital that employees of the acquired company are fully part of the process, and realize that their contribution is key to the successful integration process.

Define integration team organization

Setting up a good integration team is very similar to a recruitment process. Just as in any recruitment process, the people hired must know what is expected of them; what are the tools they can use to achieve (clearly communicated) objectives; what is the scope of that decision making; how much of a free hand they have in the areas for which they are responsible; what are the deadlines they have to meet; and to whom they report.

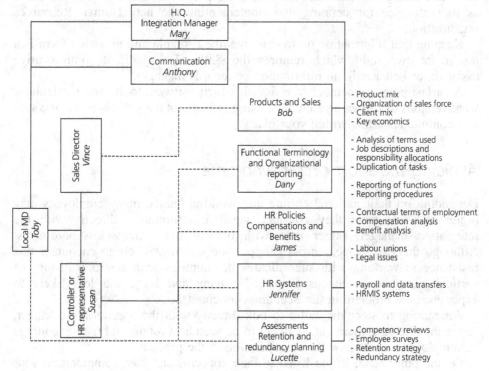

Figure 1   Sample organization chart of the integration team

If you have taken the trouble to establish a thorough integration plan, you will save a lot of time and effort. Not only will it guide you through the process itself, but also serve as a job description, an hourglass, and a family tree of those working for you.

As a last recommendation, make sure that the integration organization chart includes your team leaders' roles, and indicates particular entitlements to receive restricted or sensitive information. This should be communicated throughout the merging organizations.

Ideally, you should include with it a full contact list with the names, telephone numbers and e-mail addresses of all the integration managers, including those who are not in your team but working on other parts of the integration (such as Finance, IT, Marketing, and so on).

Organizing documentation

Within days of starting the integration process, you will be handling vast amounts of data which will not only be the source for your future comparison analyses, but also provide you with the necessary information to identify warning signals, communicate timely and appropriate information bulletins, and prepare the basis for future changes or amendments to specific situations. Ultimately, it will serve as the reference for defining and implementing the new Human Resources organization.

Keeping that information up to date, readily available and in usable form is a job in its own right which requires the skills of a qualified administrative assistant, or better still, an information or records manager.

As a last point, remember to establish which software tools, and particularly what versions of software you will be using throughout the process and make sure you communicate this within your plan.

Avoiding the short circuit syndrome

Depending on their national culture and working habits, many employees may prefer to share what they consider sensitive information directly with the integration manager, rather than with one of the manager's subordinates. Although this can happen across Europe, you are most likely to encounter this resistance to working with subordinates in countries with a strong history of vertical hierarchies, such as France, Germany and Italy, and less likely to experience the problem in the Scandinavian countries.

Attempting to steer the caller to talk directly with the appropriate manager, rather than hearing them out, is likely to be seen as a rebuff and may encourage the employee to withdraw their cooperation to the process.

On the other hand, if you listen to their concerns and then communicate your conclusions and course of action to your integration team leader, you run the risk of:

- Becoming quickly snowed under with the calls of well-intentioned employees, who should be talking to their team leaders, rather than to you. Getting your secretary to redirect these calls just makes things worse
- Destroying the credibility of your team leaders and undermining their ability to fulfill their role
- Short circuiting the information flow throughout the integration process.

One approach is to listen to your caller and respond with something like this:

> Thank you very much for this valuable information which I have taken a note of. As you know, Mr/Ms X is the integration team leader for your group and the expert for handling these kinds of issues. In order to make sure that the information that you have provided me with is given proper attention, I will forward it to Mr/Ms X and ask them to call you in order to go over the points again in detail, to check that I haven't missed anything.
>
> Mr/Ms X have full responsibility for this part of the project and, as such, can be entrusted with the most sensitive information relating to it. In the meantime, should you think of any other information relevant to the integration process, please don't hesitate to contact Mr/Ms X directly.

The benefit of this approach is that it will spare the caller's feelings and also:

- Confirm the empowerment of your team leader(s) and, in particular, give them the chance to establish a relationship with the caller (and often the caller's colleagues too)
- Give you the chance to show your team leader(s) that they are fully in command (a motivating factor), as well as an opportunity to check up on how effectively they follow-up and handle such situations
- Last, but not least, there's a strong chance that if you and your team leader handle the situation effectively, you will have solved a potential people problem and succeeded in ensuring an effective information flow.

Define the basis and timelines for reporting

There is more to effective reporting than setting up regular meetings to summarize findings and conclusions. Although an integration organization chart (Figure 1), will indicate standard direct and dotted reporting lines, don't forget this is only a chart, and no matter how detailed and self-explanatory it may be, it needs to be managed and monitored closely if you want it to work properly.

Team leaders should *report only on issues within the scope of their assignment*. This of course does not mean that they should never communicate during those meetings concerns, tips, or useful information in other areas; but as a rule, it should be made clear that whenever possible, such information should be passed over to the competent team leaders before, and independently, of a plenary meeting. Managing this properly will not only avoid frictions between your team leaders, but will also ensure the coherence and relevance of information streams and maintain the sound structure of your global plan.

Many books have been written on how to conduct successful meetings and I will not waste your time here with my own thoughts on the subject. I would, however, like to provide you with one tip I have found useful when conducting such teams:

- Request a pre-report from each team leader, *a day or two before each regular meeting*, outlining in bullet form the key areas of concern. This not only paves the way to a well-structured meeting, but also helps manage issues such as those described in the paragraph above, serves as a base to identify the need for one-on-one meetings, allows you to monitor progress and follow-up of sensitive areas, and ultimately saves a lot of time on ongoing follow-up calls.

Figure 2 is a sample reporting form that will help with the management of information and priorities. Of course, further integration reports will be much more complete than this one and detail each topic as described in the integration plan, supported by appropriate documentation.

Examples of such forms and checklists are provided in the following chapters and in Appendix 2.

Pre-reporting form

Team		Team leader					
Date		Phone number					
Country	Key issues	Potential risk/liability		Urgency	Next step	By (date)	Status
General comments:							

Figure 2   Sample reporting form

Summary

To ensure coherence and time-effective management in your process:

- Establish a detailed integration plan outlining the key topics to be addressed
- Appoint integration managers to address those key topics
- Organize the reporting and documentation management
- Build contingencies into your plan.

Prepare the communication plan

There are few people who would argue that the quality of internal communication is one, if not *the* key component to the success of an M&A integration process. Whether your company has a communication manager or not, you are the one who will be in the spotlight of one of the most sensitive communication objectives: ensuring employee commitment and loyalty – *at that very period in time* when the basis for such commitment and loyalty may be considerably weakened.

Empowering a communication team leader

Sharing the objectives of the acquisition, discussing market share, stock price, presenting the strengths and synergies of the new organization may sound like communication, but in fact is nothing more than circulating information in the 'tell' mode.

In his book *Emotional Capital*,[2] Kevin Thompson defines six levels of internal communication, spanning the gamut from Tell, Sell, Buy, Buy-In, Friends and Best-Friends modes.

Table 3 can be of help to define the current mode you are in and can be linked to the desired effect and 'tone' you are looking for.

Effective communication, especially when related to HR, is ideally a mix of messages from the above, crossing the entire spectrum from Tell to Best Friends, going beyond breaking news and also acting as a tool to soothe individual emotions and fears, silencing rumours and gossip, and preparing solid foundations for a new structure.

The success of your communication will largely depend on the frequency of internal notes, memos and progress reports. Experience indicates that beyond content, applying the following guidelines will help make your communication plan work:

a) One (and only one) communications person should write any communication, ideally for both companies. Alternatively, one person from each company should write any communication in a single voice.

2 Kevin Thompson (1998) *Emotional Capital*, Capstone Publishing Ltd.

Table 3   *The six communication modes*

Mode	Type of communication	Strengths and weaknesses
1. Tell mode	Newsletters, team briefings, manuals, policies, policies/procedures, memos, bulletin boards, guides, and e-mails.	'Tell' mode gives little opportunity for dialogue or feedback. 'Tell' alone is not enough as an internal communication. It is good for speed, but its major weakness is that it does nothing to achieve buy-in, or to take the pulse of an organization.
2. Sell mode	Team briefings, presentation skills, company magazines, videos, road shows, conferences, screen savers and push technology.	Much like making external sales, when in 'Sell', your communication style becomes more sophisticated because customers (staff) make a purchase decision as to whether or not they believe what you say.
3. Buy mode	Includes workshops, attitude surveys, and breakout sessions.	Processes to allow employees and customers to voice opinions and concerns.
4. Buy-in mode	Project meetings, town hall meetings, management and employee forums, talk backs, MBWA,[3] internal web pages, discussion groups, and employee hotlines.	Buy-in mode helps you achieve more two-way communication, face-to-face with interactive elements – builds understanding, commitment and relationships.
5. Friends mode	Psychometric surveys, breakfast sessions, and team meetings.	Just when two friends meet, people listen and respect each other. They listen to understand and to give feedback, which is what Friends mode is all about.
6. Best-friends mode	This includes 360° feedback, psychometric surveys, face-to-face meetings and customized electronic media.	When best friends meet, they listen and learn, give advice and take feedback. In the M&A integration world, it is a highly personal, highly interactive communication mode – that makes greater use of electronic media tools to gather perceptions and needs of those internal/external customers.

b) Ensure that specific communication notes are drafted to appropriate professional communities. Although general progress reports are important individuals need to be informed about the particular issues which are close to their business units, professions and personal concerns.

c) Don't forget that although most of your managers within Europe may speak English fluently, the same may not necessarily apply to all your employees. Ensuring that communication is delivered in local language – or the language of local immigrant workers – is a vital step to give people the feeling that management includes all employees, at all levels of the organization, and calls for their support and sense of belonging in the integration plan.

---

3 MBWA: **M**anagement **B**y **W**alking **A**round.

I am not suggesting that your communications manager must be proficient in all European languages. But even where translations are required, he or she should nevertheless be in control of the process and particularly of its distribution.

Since communication will include information on other aspects of the integration – such as merging technology, finance, products, etc. – you may experience overlap on a number of issues. For example, finance may be also involved in the integration of payroll systems, sales in the definition of commission plans, and IT in the merging of HRIS. Some countries or units may be faced with severe headcount reduction measures where others are not at all affected.

You may feel that in the context of an international deal involving several locations, different languages and distinct operations, setting up a communication plan is hardly realistic for one person to handle alone.

However many people are involved, the concept is that all communication must speak with a single voice. And this single voice must set the rules, tone and content regarding:

- What is being communicated and how is it structured?
- Who drafts the communication?
- Who communicates what (the CEO? the local Managing Director? Line Managers?)
- To whom is it communicated?
- What communication tools (memo, e-mail, meeting, video, intranet, and internet) will be used?
- When can it be released and who authorizes the release?
- What further action may be needed after the communication is released?

Whether the above is done by an internal or external communications expert, the CEO themselves, or a specially appointed individual, is not important. However, ensuring that all managers who have a communication role (or believe they have) adhere to this 'single voice' rule is vital for the quality, consistency and credibility of communication throughout the process.

It is essential to establish a well-defined communication process and policy and to appoint a seasoned professional to lead it.

HR communication milestones and key stakeholders

One of the first things your communications manager could do is define a global communication agenda and then review it both with the CEO and each integration manager. It is more than likely that he or she will ask you either to prepare an HR communications agenda to be integrated into their plan, or provide the content for newsletters, reports or other communication. It is also probable that they will leave it more or less up to you to decide on:

- Frequency (weekly newsletter, *ad hoc*, etc.)
- Form (newsletters, memos, conference calls, meetings, etc.), and
- Style.

A global communication integration plan will include all individuals, clients, suppliers, corporations, press and media, government agencies, etc. with a vested interest in the acquisition. Communication will focus on information given to and received from staff. However, employees are not the only stakeholders of HR communication as you can see in the sample HR communication stakeholder checklist in Table 4.

I have often heard managers say 'We will communicate as soon as we have something new to say'. Although a reasonable comment at first sight, this approach underestimates how much people want to know about things that have not yet changed, or have not been decided upon or where there is simply nothing new to report. Basically, they want to be sure that nothing has happened that they would want to know about and that may not have been communicated.

If nothing major has elapsed between your last internal communiqué, it is advisable to draft a memo summarizing past events and stating that no new events have arisen during the past period.

As a last point, regularity of communication is just as important as frequency, if not more so. Knowing that every second Monday a newsletter will be issued is reassuring. When linked to an intranet or mailbox question board, regular communication proves an invaluable tool to address questions in a global, clear and open manner.

The form and style of communication are less important provided they remain consistent (i.e. using the same form throughout the process). This is discussed in greater detail in the section headed 'Defining communication tools', p. 34.

Nevertheless, there is no question that appropriate and timely communication to the staff remains the most significant issue throughout the whole process.

Table 4   *Example HR communication stakeholder checklist*

Audience	Topic
Employees	Job security, impact on role, salary and benefits, transition terms, etc.
Unions and employee representatives	Impact on headcount, severance policies, safety, policies and regulations
Health and Accident Insurance Providers	Transfer of plans
Pension Funds Companies	Transfer, merging and funding issues
Company car suppliers	Transfer of lease ownership, change in policies
Government agencies	Termination procedure and timeline
HR software providers	Licences, transfer consulting needs, cancellations
Consultants	Ongoing contracts, recruitment and temporary staff agreements; other agreements

Milestones in HR communication

There are two main milestones to HR integration communication, and a number of points to remember.

Milestone 1: Announcing the deal

Your company may choose to have two or more announcements. The first designed for the press and shareholders, and a second, which may be more generous with explanations and rationale, designed for internal use. As both of these will be examined with the same scrutiny by employees and union representatives the following basic rules may help avoid misinterpretation, unnecessary fears and rumours.

- Make sure that the communication is given to everybody at the same time. If you are working in a multi-site environment, and have decided against an electronic messaging approach, you will have to organize the announcement agenda with your local Managing Directors
- You may have to manage the risk of internal leaks and rumours, so keeping the 'news' within a small circle of senior managers is essential. They should rely on you, and the communications specialist to give the green light to communicate. With multiple versions of announcements floating around there is potential for misinterpretation. Label **drafts** as such, and use embargoes to coordinate times and dates. Be careful of time zone changes across continents and countries even in Europe
- Make sure that people whose mother tongue is not that of the communiqué may have access to a translated version
- If you have decided on a verbal communication, it is vital to follow it up with a written summary and that people who were not able to attend the speech receive a copy of the transcripts immediately. In some instances a letter to all employees from the CEO would be appropriate
- Since all announcements of this nature will inevitably stir emotions and trigger questions, you may find it useful to set up a Q&A telephone or e-mail help desk following the announcement.

As a last general recommendation, communiqués which address downsizing and redundancy issues should not only be reviewed by the local legal counsel, but should also include some mention that whatever actions may be taken in the future, they will be done in consultation and according to local labour legislation and best practice.

You will want to create a set of communication guidelines for all managers around the time of the deal with elements such as those covered in Figure 3.

**Local market units, partners, and board members must
adhere to the following conditions:**

---

1. The offering, evaluation, pricing, forecasts, or projections should not be the subject of comment.
2. There must be no disclosure of any financial information to media or analysts.
3. There must be no disclosure of information that may be considered as key figures to the media unless approved by HQ.
4. There must be no comment on issues that may have group-wide implications or may affect share price in any way.
5. Forecasts of sales and earnings worldwide or by region or country, may not be made either in percentage or monetary terms.
6. Sales, profits, or margins worldwide or by region or country are never discussed. This may mean for instance that no weekly/monthly or quarterly sales figures are disclosed.
7. Unapproved plans for new operations, geographical areas, products, or any other rumours (for example new joint ventures, acquisitions, restructuring, personnel changes, etc.) should not be discussed. Respond to these questions by saying: 'We make it a policy not to discuss rumours'.
8. Data on the market share for any product, product line, division, operation or country may not be disclosed. Reporters may have access to rough market share information from industry associations or market studies. They might cite numbers from these sources and ask you to confirm the numbers. You should neither confirm nor deny the numbers. 'It is our company policy not to comment on figures which are not officially public.'
9. Pricing, specific product strategies, customers, and or other competitive information should not be discussed.

Figure 3   Communication guidelines

Additional specific rules to keep in mind are:

1. All contacts, statements and external communication regarding the deal *MUST* be cleared and coordinated by the communications manager. Only the designated spokespeople should respond to press or other enquiries relating to the offering.
2. No information, not already disclosed in external material, can be communicated.
3. Make sure a list of designated spokespeople is available, including their telephone numbers, names, and contact information.

Milestone 2: Communicating the integration plan

Once the deal is announced, employees will want to know the next steps. This is not only true for HR, but also for the integration of products, systems and other resources.

Since an integration plan is not a rigid structure and may evolve according to circumstances, I would avoid making an internal announcement (addressed to all employees) detailing its full structure and step-by-step approach. You should, however, communicate the following information:

- Who is responsible for the HR integration
- Details of the team that has been put in place, with their respective roles, responsibility and contact information (telephone, e-mail, etc.)
- What immediate actions will be taken (for example, review of compensation and benefit practices) and how any findings will be communicated and handled
- What the ultimate objective of these actions are, and be reassuring by explaining how these actions should help the two merging organizations offer their employees a superior working environment.

As you progress in the plan, this approach will be repeated as each new step is reached.

Further milestones: Communicate, communicate, communicate!

As you move on in the plan, you will have to decide in discussion with your communication manager what may or may not be communicated. You will also have to define what information needs to be widespread and what should be restricted to selected groups of people. As a rule of thumb, and particularly when it comes to HR communication, there are few issues about which information should be restricted. The exception to this rule is any information that will unquestionably have a damaging effect on individuals or the company.

An intranet site common to the two companies should be prepared and launched on day one. It is also a good idea to have a written document about each company to be able to acquaint staff about the other company. Such simple techniques will move you past the simple Tell mode and into the Best Friends arena, gaining support and understanding for your plan.

It is a known fact that, when faced with evasive information in times of uncertainty, many employees will first conclude that the reasons for such elusiveness is necessarily based on negative scenarios. They then feel compelled to share and compare their thoughts with fellow colleagues. As a result, the rumours and gossip which follow will nourish fears and anxieties, with the devastating effect of casting a long-lasting light of mistrust on senior management once the information is finally released – a feeling of mistrust which will be extremely difficult to reverse in the future.

The following are a few examples of essential issues you should be prepared to communicate globally, immediately, as they present themselves:

- Any changes in management, whether resignations or new appointments
- Changes in reporting lines
- Decisions to cease a product or service line, transfer a department or unit, or cease a line of operations

- Expected downsizing or redundancies, including a presentation of the relevant plan
- News and press releases, with your comments on both positive and negative feedback that might be reported in the press.

If the company is publicly traded, some of these changes must be reported externally to the shareholders. As such, coordination between internal and external communication managers needs to be well planned and bring into play the CEO, CFO, Chairman of the Board, investment bankers and so on.

The frequency and regularity of communication (ideally weekly) is just as important as the content of any communication. If there is nothing new to communicate in a given week, it is better to simply communicate just that, rather than to expect people to interpret your silence as such.

Whatever you do, if your communication (particularly if made simultaneously on announcement day) involves several steps or several people, *make sure to have an agenda ready* which you will share with all parties involved.

Table 5 is an example of an agenda used during a recent acquisition that covers the main points.

Materials to be included in briefing packs for Managing Director (MDs)

- External announcement   → Distribute to all employees as requested
- Welcome kit   → Distribute to all MDs
- Suggested speech script   → Distribute to all MDs
- Press policy   → Distribute to MDs/marketing managers
- Customer letter suggestion   → Send to customers, use as guideline in countries where the telephone is the preferred communication tool
- Q&A   → Distribute to all MDs
- Key points to be emphasized in → Distribute to all MDs
  all communications

Defining communication tools

In today's world, where the means of communication are so varied, you may easily shift from Tell to Buy and then to Friends mode, using electronic, paper or video-supported communication tools according to your needs. The choice will largely depend on your company's culture, technical sophistication, communication style, budget and resources. Nevertheless, consistency in the choice of media used is extremely important and deserves thought.

Table 5   *Acquisition agenda*

Outline Announcement Schedule		Date: April 4		
Day	Time/Location	What	Who	Status
March 27		Board meeting	CEO	
March 28		Draft announcements	Comms	
March 29–30		Draft announcements approved	Comms	
March 29–30		Prepare briefing documents	CFO, COO, HR, Comms	
April 3	Off-site	Managing Director conference	CEO, HR, MDs	
April 4	During the day	MDs arrange for local discussions at all sites	MDs	
April 4	10:00/20:00	Board phone conference for go-ahead on policy	CEO, CFO	
April 5	06:00	Send out briefing package to MDs and management	Comms Embargoed press release	
April 5	08:30	Announcement to agency online	Comms	
April 5	08:40	Follow-up call	Comms	
April 5	08:45	Agency releases to markets, to international press and wire services, Stock Exchange, Board, major investors		
	08:50	PR follow-up call, post to company website		
April 5	09:00	MDs meet with their staff	MDs	
April 5	End of day	Press clippings to MDs and management		
April 5–6	10:00–12:00	Follow-ups, where necessary with local 1:1's and international media	CEO, CFO, HR, Comms	
April 6	08:00	CEO update	CEO	
April 6	End of day	Press clippings to MDs, Company's management		
Other dates FYI				
April 13–16		Easter break in most countries		
After April 10		Annual reports sent		
May 9		Q1 results		
May 16		Annual General Meeting		

Consistency is the key to much of the process; consistency in style, consistency in frequency; consistency in selected audiences; and now consistency in media support.

When receiving information in today's 'sound bite' generation, especially from their own company, most people expect to receive news in a similar fashion as they would when reading a newspaper or listening to the radio. If on day one you use the intranet, and the next day you send out a written memo, and the third day you have recourse to e-mail, besides getting your people utterly confused, you will quickly find them spending more time looking for information they believe they might have missed, on every media support the company has to offer, rather than relying on what they receive. Once again, this may open the door to unwanted rumours and gossip.

Table 6 provides examples of topics and media support which are most often used in a communication plan.

Of course you may choose different media to address different subjects. But if you have decided that new appointments will be communicated by e-mail, that

Table 6   *Examples of topics and media support*

Issue	Media	Event	General meeting	Restricted meeting	One-on-one meeting	Video conference	Telephone conference	Update	Regular newsletter	Personal letter	Flyer	Intranet	e-mail	How-to tool kit	Other
Major announcement															
General announcements															
Select audience announcements															
CEO updates															
HR updates															
New appointments															
Resignations															
Structural changes															
Communication guidelines															
Transitional policies															
Policy changes															
HR general issues															
Redundancy/Downsizing															
Q&A															
Helpdesk support															
Other stakeholder communications															
Other															

integration progress reports will be supported on the intranet and that CEO updates will be distributed through newsletters, stick to this. And try to make sure that your approach is consistent with the approach of integration managers in other parts of the process as well.

Developing Question and Answer and communication guidelines

Since communication will play a crucial role in the transition success, one of the greatest challenges is to include goals and tasks in this transition phase. An integration process comprises specific goals that need to be met, stumbling blocks that must be overcome, and deadlines that have to be respected. And these points need to be clearly communicated as a general challenge for all involved.

The golden rules shown in Box 1 provide a simple checklist to monitor the organization's climate during the transition process.

Box 1: Golden rules for communication during mergers and acquisitions

1. Make sure you achieve a genuine consensus and buy-in for your priorities. Create common goals everyone believes in.
2. Perform a daily 10-minute process-check to review activities and priorities. Communicate effectively by communicating daily. Don't let things build up!
3. Provide positive feedback based on direct observation about what's working well. Make feedback specific and concrete. Give examples of what's working well!
4. Show willingness to reach closure in problem solving. Address the small issues and be flexible in trying various solutions. Make this a win-win process. Take turns being 'leader' and 'follower'.
5. Remain adaptable to avoid becoming stuck in non-productive behaviour patterns. Do something different. Make small experimental changes and experience how these can shift your perceptions and actions.
6. Commit to create, not to compete during the transition process. The key objective is to build an efficient new organization, and not to determine who was doing better than whom in the past. Validate the roles of others by listening and acting supportively when comparing alternative paths to follow.
7. Listen carefully and offer honest feedback when conflicts arise. Be courageous! Telling the truth when a conflict arises means eliminating more serious problems later. Be honest and be respectful. Don't attack.
8. Openly acknowledge and appreciate everyone's contributions. An 'attitude of gratitude' goes a long way. Be generous with your partners.
9. Schedule weekly time alone away from home and work. Be willing to get away from your familiar environment. Make the time as simple or as elaborate as you wish and as your means allow, but get fresh air.
10. Take immediate ownership when wrong – this strengthens processes in your business and personal relationships.

No matter how efficient your communication plan is, you will unavoidably be confronted with questions from your staff as the example in Box 2 illustrates.

Box 2: Beauty is in the mind of the beholder

In the announcement which followed the acquisition of a Swedish software company, it was proudly trumpeted that all operational units would be fully integrated in the new structure and that every member of the support and administrative units would get fair interviews and be given priority for whatever vacancies the acquiring company had, in their respective areas of expertise.

Within a week, all staff of the operational units had received a written offer of employment which the acquiring company thought of as 'unique career opportunities'. The remaining staff had interviews scheduled, and the interviewers were fully briefed and supported by a Q&A kit to help them answer questions from applicants.

It was taken for granted, however, that members of the operational units would be so pleased to join an international company with pan-European presence, and so relieved to have employment security, that the employment offers would automatically be gratefully received. As a result, no additional guidance was given to the operational unit managers who would be integrating the expected newcomers.

Questions abounded! From reporting issues, managerial responsibilities, operational practices, to product definitions, managers were plied with questions which they answered to the best of their ability, but with their own vision of the new organization, which, by the nature of things, was open to different interpretations.

Panic struck when the two key unit managers of the acquired company declined the offers, which in turn triggered a chain reaction of support from their own employees in both units.

A crisis team was put together, this time with the appropriate set of instructions, guidelines, and Q&A in order to reach consensus. Although consensus was ultimately achieved, the power play had shifted sides. What should have been the smooth, easy and positive merging of two groups of complementary professionals turned out to be *the* victory of one team against the other in a situation where there should have been no grounds for a battlefield in the first place.

Time soothed the wounds, and the acquisition was finally and successfully completed. However, the cost, emotional strain and internal politics that it generated, left a scar which could easily have been avoided.

The moral of this is that what may appear to you a great deal, may be perceived differently by those for whom it is intended. Don't take for granted that things which may appear intellectually unquestionable, will remain unquestioned by all employees, or that whatever you are saying will be automatically accepted as unquestionable.

As a result, you will want to help your managers to address questions they don't necessarily have the answers to, and also provide them with the answers that can be given in some specific situations.

Start by setting up a 'general set of guidelines for communication', particularly when faced with a multi-site acquisition and where local managing directors may be faced with the press requiring statements. Such a briefing pack should include at the very least:

1. Key points to be emphasized in all communications. This is your opportunity to help sell the deal.

2. The press policy which all staff are required to follow and a copy of the press release(s).
3. A Q&A sheet addressing general HR issues, competition and strategy, and financial statements.
4. A proposed speech for the MDs to give their staff.
5. The timing of releases with an outline schedule.

Depending on the speed of the integration and how communications will be grouped, you should also include at some stage:

1. A new employee welcome kit.
2. A termination guidelines kit (see Chapter 4, Part III, on terminations).

Both of these should include a Q&A briefing document.

Q&A's can generally be divided into two main categories:

1. Business questions relating to the deal itself.
2. HR questions relating to organization, compensation and benefits.

See Box 3 for the 10 key rules of the Communication Code of Conduct at all times.

Box 3: The Communication Code of Conduct

1. Never discuss something you don't know the answer to. If you don't know, or aren't sure, it's quite OK to say 'I don't know' or 'Let me find out and get back to you'.
2. Do not hide or camouflage information you are supposed to communicate because you fear negative feedback. For the sake of short time peace of mind, you will earn a month of bitterness and mistrust from your people when they find out. And invariably they will.
3. Don't lie.
4. Don't make promises you cannot keep.
5. Remain factual – don't attempt to make things look better than they are. People prefer to receive a straightforward and honest piece of information, even if it includes disturbing news, than have the feeling they are being given sweeteners to cover the bitterness of reality.
6. Listen – don't systematically comment – to questions or concerns, but follow-up on them at the appropriate time.
7. Don't expect people to interpret silence as the absence of news. Provide regular feedback, and if there is nothing new to communicate on feedback day, hold the meeting anyway. Be available for questions.
8. Whatever your personal opinions may be, keep them to yourself.
9. Keep people focused on business goals.
10. Remain available. Make room in your agenda for one-on-one meetings, as some people will need to share their emotions and questions with you on a personal basis.

Box 4 and Box 5 provide some examples of the questions you need to prepare for:

Box 4: Business questions relating to the deal itself

- What's in it for me?
- We weren't doing so badly, was this acquisition really necessary?
- Is this deal designed to increase market share by uniting forces or by eliminating a competitor?
- How will the new strategy affect our product offering, pricing, marketing and corporate identity?
- How will this affect current operational spending and budgets, particularly in marketing, product development and support?
- Will the company have another name? How do we answer the phone in the meantime?
- How will this affect the organization structure and current reporting lines?
- Will certain areas of activity be centralized and how will it affect us?
- Will any plants/units be closed and what redundancies are foreseen?
- How do we handle overlapping customers, particularly where we compete on comparable products?
- How will this affect our suppliers?
- In locations where we both are present but where we are bigger and more successful than our acquirer, will they be integrating with us or will we be integrating with them?
- Are we one out of many acquisitions the acquirer intends to make this year and if so, what can we expect in the short and medium term?

Box 5: HR questions relating to organization, compensation and benefits

- Will I still report to the same manager?
- Will I still have the same title and responsibilities?
- Will I still have the same customers, products, territory?
- How will this affect my current compensation? Will we have a new commission system?
- Will we keep our current benefits or will new plans be set up? What will they be?
- How does the deal affect pension plans, health insurance, etc.?
- I am about to start a long-term training programme sponsored by the company. Is this commitment affected in anyway by the deal? Will any other commitments be cancelled?
- How does the deal affect my stock-option programme? Can I exercise all of my unvested options as a result of the deal?

- How does the deal affect my bonus objectives? If a new bonus plan is to be put in place, when will it be effective and how will my bonus be calculated for the period before and after the deal?
- If I decide to leave the company now, is my non-competition clause still valid?
- If my position is subject to be suppressed or transferred and I decide to leave before a final decision is made, will I still be entitled to some form of compensation or severance pay? How do I get information on this?
- Will my rights to holiday and overtime be transferred and accrued in the new company, or will it be paid for *in lieu* with a 'back to zero' policy?
- Where can I find out about new vacancies and challenges in the new organization?
- How and when will the redundancy process start? Will there be assessments? Who will conduct them?
- Is my work contract still valid? Do special agreements (such as fixed terms, exceptional bonuses, sabbatical leaves) still apply?

Summary

Communication is a key factor to the success of the integration process.

It requires:

- An empowered communications leader
- Clear guidelines of who can communicate what, when and to whom
- A consistent approach in communication tools used for transmitting information
- A thorough preparation of Q&A's
- And above all, straightforward, timely, honest, clear and regular flow of information.

Note on cultural integration

In many books and articles addressing workforce integration, you will find various analyses and advice on how to merge cultures in an integration process.

I have deliberately avoided the subject considering that attempts *to merge cultures* (whether corporate or human) in a short and predetermined timeframe, has a lot in common with trying to blend mustard, oil and vinegar. Whip those ingredients up properly, and the mix will probably look good. Let it rest for a moment and witness how they start to part from each other only minutes after they are left alone.

This is of course a simple example but there is one lesson to learn by it: will the looks of the dressing alter the taste of the dish if left alone?

In Europe, vast cultural differences exist, and the key to successful integration is first to be aware of them, and second to understand how they can best be used in the organization. Attempting to 'force' cultural integration in record time is a waste of money and resources.

And what about corporate culture, you may ask? Reading most annual reports, you will find that corporations boast about their culture originating at the date of foundation. In other words, it was built over time, and experience, with successes and mistakes. The same applies to the success of the cultural integration of two corporations. It takes time.

Part II
The transition period

A people that values its privileges above its principles soon loses both.

Dwight D. Eisenhower (1890–1969)

This section will cover how to:

- Compare terms of employment
- Analyse differences in compensation and benefits
- Define HR data transition
- Assess corporate handbooks and procedures
- Secure and retain key employees

Chapter 1

Analysis and comparison of terms of employment

In this chapter, we will analyse and compare compensation and benefits, identify potential areas of concern, and discover how to try and unify both companies' systems into one unified product.

Depending on the country you are working in today, you may question the need to go through this detailed comparison, arguing that at the end of the day, compensation and benefits will be what they are, and that employees will have no choice other than to 'take it or leave it'.

There are two major flaws to this reasoning, the first emotional, the second legal. Emotionally, employees are going through a transition phase, and as we have seen earlier, will be extremely sensitive to any change in their current employment packages. With their loyalty weakened at a time when it is most needed, adjusting the compensation and benefits package is a delicate issue which, if properly managed, can be used greatly to the company's advantage; but if poorly handled, can trigger unwanted resignations. Legally, member states of the European Union in particular have implemented the concept of *acquired rights*. In other words, if the company offers a number of benefits (whether or not specifically expressed in the employment contract), for instance additional medical coverage, or pension plans, or company cars, etc., they become an 'acquired right' (and not a *pro gratia* benefit). As a result, employees have a legal claim to maintain such benefits after a merger, acquisition or whatever event is affecting the company's corporate structure and regulations. Changes to such benefits can only be made with the agreement of all staff (and usually their representatives) and in most instances should present, directly or indirectly, an improvement to their current situation.

In any event, you might find it useful to distribute a Q&A on these issues, or at least be prepared to answer questions such as those posed in Box 1.

Box 1: Compensation and Benefits Questions and Answers

- How will my title and salary be affected after the merger?
- Will I continue to be paid on a bi-monthly basis?
- How will the new commission system work? What changes will affect me?
- I should be having my performance and salary review next month. How does the merger affect this process?
- I had a salary review last month and my salary should be adjusted next quarter. Is this still valid?
- Will our year-end bonuses be affected?
- I have several hours of overtime, under which overtime policy will I get paid?
- When will the new weekly schedule be implemented?
- I am paid on an hourly basis according to a 40-hour week. The acquiring company has a 38-hour week. Does that mean my salary will be reduced proportionally?
- My family is covered by the company's health insurance. Will this change?
- Will the special pension plan scheme be maintained?
- What happens to my stock options? Will there be a new stock option plan?
- I have holidays scheduled next month, can I take them?

Analysis of differences in contractual terms of employment

The analysis of contractual terms of employment will focus on the two following key issues:

1. The employment contract.
2. Salary and commission systems.

The comparison of corporate benefits is a separate topic that will be addressed further in this chapter.

The employment contract

This analysis is generally performed in two steps:

1. Management's contractual terms of employment.
2. General contractual terms of employment.

Although in many European countries, the existence of a written employment contract is not a legal obligation, it is the general practice for both managerial and general staff, and should undoubtedly be the course to follow in an M&A process.

The analysis of management's contractual terms of employment is normally carried out during the Due Diligence process. The process is generally limited to top management as its main objective is to highlight potential financial liabilities, particularly when considering the set-up of the new management team and the redundancies or resignations which invariably follow. In any event, it should be performed with care and in detail as it touches the most sensitive issues relating to employee loyalty.

The general terms of employment will focus more, as its name indicates, on general terms.

Key issues to assess in senior management contractual terms of employment include:

- Global remuneration (including fringe benefits)
- Notice periods
- Contractual severance agreements
- Vesting rights on stock options
- Share ownership
- Non-competition clauses.

The approach is similar to the one used in the compensation and benefits analysis described later in this chapter, although it is more specific and in-depth, as illustrated by the examples in Table 1.

As it is more than likely that each member of senior management will have individual and specific agreements, this exercise needs to be repeated for each position under examination.

Key issues to assess in general contractual terms of employment

---

Normally, the comparative analysis described earlier should cover the issues for the majority of employees. However, it is useful to establish whether:

- Each employee has an employment contract
- Some employees have clauses, which differ widely from the general practice, or represent potential liabilities.

Be also particularly careful in examining any general usages, or agreements existing between the company and temporary personnel, consultants or any form of workers on outsourcing contracts.

The approach is identical to the one for senior management.

Note: Special agreements relating to extended holiday rights, part-time employment, training agreements and so forth do not really fit in this sort of analysis and should be discussed on a one-to-one basis later in the process.

Table 1   *Analysis of corporate contractual liabilities, senior management*

Function: Senior V.P. Int'l Sales

Agreement	Company A	Company B
Global remuneration	€200,000 base salary €100,000 bonus based on performance, pro gratiae bonus on company performance	€230,000 base salary €100,000 bonus based on performance
Notice period	6 months	6 months
Contractual severance agreements	2 additional months for each year of service (with full compensation benefit rights, i.e. pension, health, etc.) 100% of bonus during the full severance period €250,000 additional flat indemnity	2 years salary (including bonus) for every completed 3 years spent in the company. Paid as flat sum without access to salary-linked benefits
Vesting rights on stock options*	In case of termination as a result of an M&A, stock options are immediately vested and exercisable. Represents to date 1,000,000 shares worth €9 million with an offer price at €5 million	No vesting rights in case of M&A but a flat indemnity of €500,000 in case of termination or inability to exercise options due to an M&A or termination without fault, and provided bearer holds at least 100,000 unvested options at time of severance Holds 250,000 options of which 100,000 are vested but not exercised, worth €1.2 million with strike price at €300,000
Share ownership	2% with voting rights	Negligible
Non-competition clauses	Only in case of voluntary resignation €100,000 + 60% of global remuneration calculated on past 3 years for the following 2 years of unemployment	None

* When comparing stock option vesting rights, pay special attention to compliance with local laws. As illustrated in 'Part I: Facts with direct financial implications (hard facts)', it is not uncommon to find that corporate stock option rules and regulations which are perfectly in line with Headquarters national law do not fully comply with those of its subsidiaries.

Analysis and comparison of salary and commission systems

If HR is involved in the preliminary merger discussions, this process is normally conducted as part of the HR Due Diligence review.

When HR is not directly involved from the onset of the process, people who conducted the deal usually have only a fraction of the information focusing on major areas of potential liability. Consequently, this part of the process needs to be addressed extremely quickly once the deal is done, in order to establish, ideally within the two months following the announcement, a comprehensive and attractive new or reinforced global, compensation and benefit policy.

The major components of a compensation review are:

- Salary ranges per position
- Commission system
- Individual performance bonus and pay-out policy
- Company performance bonus (profit sharing) policy
- Overtime policy
- Salary review policies
- Frequency of payments (i.e. 12, 13, 14 or more salaries per year)
- Tax exempt payments (forfeit expenses, special arrangements).

Salary ranges per position
The approach for salary comparison per position was described previously. It will serve as a base as you proceed with the details of the package.

Commission systems
If your company has a sales force, a great deal of care must be given to the commission system analysis, as changes you may need to bring to it later affect the most sensitive and emotional issues for a salesperson:

- Individual sales targets
- Income (commission on sales)
- Commission payment frequency.

You must also remember that the commission system cannot be analysed as a totally separate item in the compensation scheme but integrated into the complete package.

Individual performance bonus policy
This should be distinguished from commission and other profit sharing schemes. Focus must be on:

- The existence of a performance assessment policy
- The financial reward calculation system used, and
- The frequency of the assessments (and rewards).

Very popular in the non-sales departments, and more often based on soft facts, the successful integration of well designed performance bonus policies often play a soothing and stabilizing role in the years following the merger.

Company performance bonus (profit sharing) policy
Here too, bonuses or premiums related to the company's performance or profits vary considerably from one country, and one company, to another. Although contractual premiums related to the company's profits are generally governed by local labour legislation,[1] the same does not apply to company performance bonuses, which are governed by corporate policies only.

1 In France, for example, companies with more than 100 employees have to introduce *a 'Réserve spéciale de participation'* a compulsory profit sharing plan.

Overtime policies

Often overlooked, overtime policies should be carefully compared. The following will deserve your special attention:

- Is overtime a generally accepted practice or does it require prior approval by a manager?
- Is overtime compensated for in a cash payment or by giving time off?
- Is there an upper limit for accruable overtime?
- Are some categories of personnel excluded from overtime compensation (i.e. senior management)?
- Does the company comply with legal requirements?

Salary review policies

It is important to ascertain both companies' policies at both corporate and individual level, i.e.

- How are yearly general salary increases performed and by whom (legally prescribed minimum, cost of living, union agreement, etc.)?
- How are individual salary reviews performed (performance appraisal basis, timing, frequency)?

And how do such practices compare between the merging entities.

Frequency of payment

Policies on the frequency of salary payments vary considerably not only from one country to another, but also from one company's philosophy to another.

The inherent differences are not limited themselves only to the quantity of salary payments within a given year, but also to payout dates and amounts.

For example, companies with a 14-month salary practice may very well decide to pay one of the additional months in June and the other in December. But others may choose the end of the year to pay all outstanding salaries, bonuses and year-end benefits. Companies may use either the calendar year or their fiscal year as a reference. Merging two companies with different practices at this level is a sensitive issue, which will be discussed later in the chapter. I recommend making a distinction between salary practices for top executive management and for the rest of the staff.

Although you will need to make a comparable analysis available when time comes to put the new top management of the company in place, what you really need to focus on at this stage are global salary practices and their idiosyncrasies, in order to implement a unified approach.

Special payments (tax-free allowances)

In some European countries, senior managers may receive a tax-free allowance for representative positions. Subject to agreements with the tax authorities, these allowances are called 'forfeit expense allowances' or simply 'tax-free representative allowances'.

These payments may represent a single lump sum payment or a payment split over several years, for reasons of tax. These allowances may represent a significant payroll liability.

Table 2 is a sample comparison form which, as you will see in the following chapters, can be fine-tuned to compare titles, functions, weightings and salary ranges, depending on the size and specifics of your organization.

As you gain more insight on the different forms proposed here, it will then be a question of personal preference on whether to use one form to address all the issues, or separate forms for specific issues.

At this stage of an M&A process, I have encountered a number of situations where either the CFO or the V.P., Human Resources have started a number of forecasts in order to appreciate the financial impact of adjustments from one system to another.

In my experience, these have little relevance unless the assessments, manpower planning, sales objectives and financial goals have already been defined.

Table 2 *Salary practice analysis*

	Company A	Company B	Minimum legal requirement	Plan
Base salary				
Management	Market average	About 10% more than Company A		Packages to be re-negotiated on individual basis
Sales staff	Market average	About 20% more than Company A		Phase out over time. Targets & commissions to reflect differences in global compensation
Support staff	Slightly above market average	Slightly below market average		No immediate change
Salary instalments	13 months (2 months paid in December)	14 months (two months paid in June and two in December)	12 months	Since Company B does not have individual performance bonuses (see below), replace the 14th month by a performance bonus. Institutionalize the same for Company A
Pay date	On 25th of each month	Every second Monday	Monthly	Introduce monthly payments for all (prepare communication plan)
	Commissions paid monthly with quarterly adjustments for bad debt	Commissions paid quarterly on collection basis	Yearly	Standardize to monthly payments with quarterly adjustments to allow smoother income for sales personnel
Pay mode	Bank transfer	Cheque	None	Payments to be made by bank transfer. Will require collecting *ad hoc* info
Commission				
Sales staff	10% of sales up to 100K / 20% of sales over 100K	€5000 per 80K sales / €3000 additional for each 150K level reached	None	Standardize plan according to new objectives
Individual performance bonus				
Sales functions	Additional €2000–€10,000 if annual target exceeded (depending on seniority and objectives set)	No additional bonus except for extraordinary circumstances	None	Introduce special superior performance bonus
Support function	10–30% of basic salary based on performance appraisal system	Left to the discretion of manager upon exceptional performance	None	Individual performance bonus linked to individual performance appraisal to be introduced throughout company

	Company A	Company B	Minimum legal requirement	Plan
Profit sharing				
Management	Discretionary	None	None	Do not institutionalize yet
Staff	None	None	None	Leave as is
Overtime policy				
Management	No compensation	No compensation	None	Leave as is
Staff	As needed. Compensated by time off	Exceptional. Needs written approval from superior. Compensated in cash or time off according to labour legislations	Between 125% and 200% either cash or time off depending on day of week and time of day	Overtime to be subject to request/approval by manager (policy to be introduced). Overtime to be compensated by time off
Salary review policy				
Management	Yearly review according to performance appraisal. Minimum increase = cost of living	Yearly review with superior	Cost of living Index is guideline	As cost of living index is no legal obligation, management's salary increase should be left to the discretion of superior on basis of performance appraisal
Staff	Yearly review. Minimum increase = cost of living	Yearly review. Minimum increase = cost of living	Cost of living Index is guideline	No change
Special payments				
Expenses for relevant staff	Tax-free and reimbursement upon receipts	Reimbursement upon receipt	Reimbursement upon receipt	Tax-free forfeit to be negotiated for all relevant staff

Chapter 2

Analysis and comparison of benefits

Dividing benefits into two distinct groups (health, pension, and related benefits, and social and other benefits) is often useful, as they require different levels of expertise and consideration.

You may find you save time and get better results by using the services of an insurance expert or actuary to get the summarized comparative picture, advantages and disadvantages of the systems of both companies being examined, and finally the financial implications in adjusting one programme with another.

If you intend to establish a corporate-wide policy covering international subsidiaries, then such advice becomes indispensable because each European country has specific social security legislation to which alternative plans can be added, but with specific *ad hoc* tuning. The European Union has issued a *Memorandum of Acquired Rights* on this issue, a copy of which is included in Appendix 2.

Whatever you decide, the following is a recommended approach to help you not only define the best path to follow, but also to be in a position to answer fully the questions employees will invariably ask on these subjects.

To illustrate what these comparative tables may look like, and to get an idea of the key items they should include, please look at the following examples based on two international companies merging operations in Switzerland. Switzerland was chosen as a case example because the Swiss social security system presents such limited basic coverage to employees, that it compels employers to provide alternative and complementary insurance in the full register of insurance, including health, disability, retirement and death. As such, this exercise presents a fairly wide range of issues to examine, and which you should be able to apply to most comparative analyses of this kind.

Health, pension and related benefits

In this subgroup, the following should be considered:

- Scope of health, accident and related medical coverage
- Old age and retirement
- Life insurance.

Scope of medical coverage

This includes a number of issues such as:

- Medical treatments insured
- Pharmaceutical expenses covered
- Hospitalization
- Loss of salary during illness/accident (including the mandatory waiting period)
- Invalidity/Disability pension.

See Tables 3, 4, 5 and 6 for a comparison of accident insurance, including medical coverage; loss of salary and invalidity coverage; a comparison of health insurance covering the same topics; a detailed comparison covering the extent of medical coverage for specific issues in case of illness; a detailed comparison covering the same in case of accident.

In most European countries, the aforementioned items are covered by the individual national social security systems, although some additional coverage may be insured – most commonly for management – for private care hospitalization. If you are conducting a pan-European merger, you should gather a thorough understanding of such local practices, as they are surprisingly different from one country to another.

Also keep in mind that in many situations, additional insurance benefits (health, life and pension in particular) are subject to separate agreements between employee and employer where the employer contributes to an additional insurance scheme. Although this has little to do with the comparison of statutory benefits itself, it should be addressed quickly with the concerned parties in order to avoid unwanted interpretations.

Old age and retirement

Old age and retirement programmes are governed by national social security rules and regulations in force in each country. Here again, an increasing amount of corporations offer additional coverage to their employees.

In many instances, such additional plans are designed primarily to represent a tax-effective differed compensation system. Nevertheless, their significance as an integral part of the negotiated compensation agreement has increased as company social benefits have improved, and they are one of the most delicate benefits to alter.

Table 3 *Comparative analysis, accident insurance, Switzerland*

	Legal minimum	Company A	Company B	Comment	Premium differential
Treatment	International coverage for essential medical treatment, surgery and hospitalization in semi-private care	Unlimited coverage world-wide for medical treatment, drugs, surgery and hospitalization in private care	Unlimited coverage world-wide for medical treatment, drugs, surgery and hospitalization in private care	Same policy	Same premium
Loss of salary	80% of salary capped at Sfr106,800 until recovery or permanent invalidity, which must be established if work incapacity lasts more than 720 days in a row	90% of insured salary as of day 1 (base + 2/3 of projected bonus) until recovery or permanent invalidity, which must be established if work incapacity lasts more than 720 days in a row	100% of insured salary as of day 1 (base without bonus) until recovery or permanent invalidity, which must be established if work incapacity lasts more than 720 days in a row	Company A includes a theoretical salary with bonus. Better plan for the sales force. Ideally, plan should cover 100% of insured salary. Cost to the company would represent a 0.1% insurance premium increase	Premium difference < 0.5%
Invalidity	Invalidity pension of 80% of LAA* based salary (Sfr106,800)	Invalidity pension of 80% of LAA* based salary	Invalidity pension of 80% of LAA* based salary	Represents the basis of the majority of plans, which are then adapted accordingly	Some initiatives are private, others relate to social security
		Additional			
		One year's insured salary in capital with a 350% progression	Two years salary (last insured salary as reference)	Company A offers a globally better coverage for its staff Differences in premiums are minimal	Premium difference < 0.75%
		Additional pension of 60% of insured salary over the LAA* maximum	Additional pension of 40% of insured salary over LAA* maximum	Advise to shift all staff to plan of Company A	
		Additional pension for every dependant child equal to 20% of insured salary over the LAA* maximum	Additional pension for every dependant of 25% of insured salary over the LAA* maximum, but max 90% of insured salary		

*Lois sur l'Assurance Accident. (Law on Accident Insurance in Switzerland)

Table 4 *Comparative analysis, health insurance, Switzerland*

	Legal minimum	Company A	Company B	Comment	Premium differential
Treatment	Basic drug and medical treatment in Canton of residence. Hospitalization in general ward. Full cost to employee	Offers employees the possibility to join a corporate plan at a discount rate. Provides flat taxable contribution of Sfr250. Extent of plan and final premiums left to the employee's discretion	Offers employees the possibility to join the company's corporate medi-plan, with full medical, drug and hospitalization coverage in private care. Premiums are borne by the company (taxable)	Company B has a particularly generous plan, going beyond general local standard. Recommend keeping plan of Company A for all future employees. Transferred employees to receive cash contribution in lieu	About Sfr350.- per employee per month
Loss of salary	According to Bern Scale 3 weeks in 1st year of employment 4 weeks in 2nd year 9 weeks in 3rd, etc.	80% of base salary as of 31st day of work incapacity and until recovery or permanent invalidity (must be established if work incapacity lasts more than 720 days in a row)	100% of insured salary as of 90th day of incapacity (base without bonus) until recovery or permanent invalidity (must be established if work incapacity lasts more than 720 days in a row)	Loss of salary in case of illness is a separate contract to the health insurance. Waiting period in Company B's plan allows for cheaper premium and better coverage	Plan B would allow premium reduction of about 0.8% on salary mass. Waiting period represents minimal financial risk. Recommend shifting to plan of Company B
Invalidity	Invalidity pension of up to 90% of capped salary (Sfr106,800)	Invalidity pension of up to 90% of capped salary (Sfr106,800)	Invalidity pension of up to 90% of capped salary (Sfr106,800)	Legal base	Some initiatives are private, others relate to social security
Additional					
		One year's insured salary in capital with a 350% progression	Two years salary (last insured salary as reference)	Company A globally offers a better coverage for its staff. Differences in premiums are minimal. Advise to shift all staff to plan of Company A	Premium difference < 0.90%
		Additional pension to government pension insuring 60% of uncapped base salary	Additional pension to government pension insuring 40% of uncapped insured salary		
		Additional pension for every dependant child equal to 20% of base salary. Total pension may not exceed 100% of base salary	Additional pension for every dependant of 25% of insured salary. Total pension may not exceed 90% of insured salary		

Table 5 *Comparative analysis, extent of coverage, health insurance*

Coverage	Legal minimum	Plan A	Plan B	Plan C
Doctor's fees	Approved doctors only in canton of residence	Approved doctors only, nationwide	International coverage	International coverage
Hospitalization	General care in approved hospital in canton of residence	General care in approved hospital in country of residence	International coverage in private care in case of emergency only	International coverage in private care in case of emergency. In other cases, requires approval of insurance company
Pregnancy and delivery	General care in approved hospital in canton of residence	General care in approved hospital in country of residence. Treatment of baby covered as well	International coverage in general care for mother and child	International coverage in private care for mother and child
Pharmaceuticals	Listed drugs only	Refund of 80% of non-listed drugs, excluding homeopathy, and alternative medication	Refund 80% of all prescribed medication	Refund 80% of all prescribed medication
Cures	Listed cures only	Approved medical treatment and contribution to accommodation up to €30 / day	Medical treatment as prescribed and contribution to accommodation up to €50 / day	Medical treatment as prescribed and contribution to accommodation up to €80 / day
Aids and prosthesis	Listed aids only	90% of prosthesis up to €300	90% of prosthesis up to €300	90% of prosthesis up to €1000
Dental	No coverage	No coverage	80% of doctor's bill Max. €1500 of treatment cost	80% of doctor bill Max. €2500 of treatment cost
Glasses and visual aids	€135 per annum	90% of doctor's bill Max. €100 of other costs	90% of doctor's bill Max. €100 of other costs	90% of doctor's bill Max. €300 of other costs
Emergency repatriation	None. Treatment to be administered locally and refunded according to legal minimum regulations	90% of repatriation cost capped at €7000 Local medical treatment and hospitalization up to 60 days	90% of search and rescue cost capped at €10,000 90% of repatriation cost capped at €20,000 Local medical treatment and hospitalization up to 60 days	90% of search and rescue cost capped at €30,000 90% of repatriation cost, uncapped Local medical treatment and hospitalization up to 60 days

Table 6　　*Sample comparative sheet, insurance policy, Switzerland*

Insured risk	Treatment	Loss of salary	Invalidity	Death
Accident	Unlimited coverage world-wide for: medical treatment, drugs, surgery and hospitalization in private care	90% of insured salary (base + 2/3 of bonus) until recovery or permanent invalidity, which must be established if work incapacity lasts more than 720 days in a row	Invalidity pension of 80% of LAA* based salary	Widow's pension of 40% of LAA* salary Orphan's pension of 15% of LAA* salary per orphan
	Unlimited coverage, world-wide		**LAA* max salary = Frs106,800**	
			One year's insured salary in capital with a 350% progression	One year's insured salary in capital
			Additional pension of 60% of insured salary over the LAA* maximum	Additional widow's pensions of 60% of insured salary over the LAA* maximum
			Additional pension for every dependant child equal to 20% of insured salary over the LAA* maximum	Additional pension for every dependant child equal to 20% of insured salary over the LAA* maximum
Illness	Coverage according to individual plan (see Intras Package). As a rule of thumb, 90% of all medical, drugs and hospitalization in private care	90% of insured salary (base + 2/3 of bonus) until recovery or permanent invalidity, which must be established if work incapacity lasts more than 720 days in a row	Pension of 60% of insured salary. Additional pension for every dependant child equal to 20% of insured salary	Pension of 60% of insured salary. Additional pension for every dependant child equal to 20% of insured salary

*Lois sur l'Assurance Accident (Law on Accident Insurance in Switzerland)

Detailed comparison of pension funds should be left to professional actuaries and fund managers.

You can get a good idea of potential areas of concern, which will then help you steer pension fund consultants and actuaries by comparing the following (see Table 7).

Table 7 *Comparative analysis, extent of coverage, pension fund, Switzerland*

Coverage	Legal minimum	Plan Company A	Plan Company B
Premiums	Between 7 and 18% of Federal established minimum Premiums vary according to age and sex and are shared equally between employer and employee	Between 8 and 12% of base salary capped at €150K Premiums are shared equally	18% of insured salary (base + 2/3 of bonus) uncapped 1/3 of premiums paid by employee and 2/3 by employer
Capitalization	Limited. Capital may be used to finance own mortgage	Full. Accrual interest of 4%. Employee may choose between capital and pension 5 years before retirement age May also cash capital if leaving the country permanently	Full + added capitalization from fund profits and minimum interest of 4.5% Employee may choose between capital and pension 5 years before retirement age May also cash capital if leaving the country permanently
Nature of benefits	6.8% of accrued capital	6.8% of accrued capital	6.8% of accrued capital
Retirement age	65 years old for men, 62 for women	Same as legal minimum, but employee may retire up to 5 years earlier	Same as legal minimum, but employee may retire up to 10 years earlier
Widows' pension	60% of pension	60% of pension	70% of pension
Orphans' pension	20% of pension but full pension may not exceed 100%	20% of pension but full pension may not exceed 100%	20% of pension but full pension may not exceed 100%
Disability	Depending on degree of invalidity, up to 90% of salary capped at Federal maximum	60% of salary (+ 20% for dependant child below 18 years), but may not be lower than 90% of Federal maximum	80% of last salary
Indexation	Cost of living index	Cost of living index	Cost of living index
Other benefits	None	Additional life insurance equal to 3.5 times annual salaries	Additional life insurance of €750K Additional disability insurance of up to €750K depending on degree of invalidity Fund will also finance mortgage at preferential rates

Note: This table is fictitious. Legal minimums are a reflection of the Swiss pension system, but for simplicity reasons, they have been considerably summarized and truncated. As a result, the example should not be used as a source of reference.

Life insurance

Life insurance is a popular benefit in a number of European countries as a form of tax-friendly deferred compensation, particularly when it includes a capitalization benefit. Although the premiums are, for the most part, paid by the employer, in some cases they are split. Some policies may include a pension in lieu of capital, and some may cover spouse and dependants, where others don't. Preparing comparative tables is therefore recommended.

Another point to keep in mind, is that in order to minimize financial losses which may result from the death of a key member of management, an increasing number of companies are taking out life insurance policies where the company itself is the beneficiary.

Table 8   *Comparative analysis of life insurance*

Coverage	Plan A	Plan B	Comments
Base coverage	Three times base salary	€200,000 for employees €350,000 for managers €500,000 for executives	
Maximum coverage	€500,000	Additional coverage possible at employee's expense	
Capitalization	2/3 of premiums are capitalized	None	
Eligibility and duration	As of first day of employment, in case of accident As of 90th day of employment in case of illness, provided illness had not been diagnosed within first 60 days Maximum duration is 25 years or until employee reaches age of 60, at which time capital is paid. 20% of capitalization vested every 5 years	Eligible after 60 days of employment, subject to entry medical check Duration of 20 years, renewable	Cancelling Plan A would mean losing vesting rights for a large number of employees
Life insurance of spouse and dependants	Not insured	Life insurance of spouse = 25% of insured capital Life insurance of child = 20% of insured capital	Cancelling Plan B would probably involve introducing coverage for dependants in the new plan
Contributions	Paid by employer	Paid by employer Additional coverage paid by employee	

Social and other benefits

The majority of corporations provide employees with a number of benefits which go beyond legally required provisions. Some of them are simply a more generous extension of labour legislation, and others are a form of privilege employees receive through working for the corporation. Seniority, function and title may also play a role in defining who is eligible for what benefit.

When dealing with companies based in Europe, some caution should be observed before deciding to suppress a benefit, particularly if these benefits are explicitly referred to in a working contract or have been granted on a continuous basis for a number of years. Labour courts often consider benefits as an acquired right, which cannot be removed without alternative forms of compensation.

Although the genuine impact that the granting of benefits may have on an employee's loyalty and motivation are far from being established, there remains little doubt that any attempt at removing them will create hardship, loss of motivation and even increase employee turnover.

Table 9 is a sample of a benefit comparison chart. The full comparative process requires going into some extra details apart from the points presented here. This is particularly true when comparing stock option plans and other profit sharing programmes.

Table 9   *Comparative benefits analysis*

Benefit	Legal requirements	Company A	Company B	Comment
Holidays	4 weeks	4 weeks for staff 5 weeks for management	5 weeks for staff 6 weeks for management	Discussion point to address quickly
Working week	45 hours / week	42.5 hours / week	40 hours / week	Recommend to introduce 40 hours as this is the industry standard
Retirement age	65 years old	65 years old. Early requirement possible at 60 years old	65 years old. Early requirement possible at 55 years old	No employee approaching retirement age. No real issue. To be discussed when merging plans
Overtime	100% compensation if performed during weekdays between 7 a.m. and 8 p.m. 125% compensation for night work or over the weekend 150% compensation for night work during the week-end	100% up to the 45th hour 125% beyond the 45th hour 150% for night work or weekends 200% for night work over weekends	According to legal minimum	Discussion point. Although a social move, paying over the odds for overtime does not seem to respond to any imperative

Benefit	Legal requirements	Company A	Company B	Comment
Profit sharing	If company greater than 100 employees, according to formula	Government formula or 0.01% of profits, whichever is greater	Government formula and *ad hoc* premiums according to individual merit and performance	To be reviewed with stock option plan
Stock option plan	None	5 year vesting Can receive up to 50% of bonus in stock Purchase plan according to management level	5 year vesting for stock options Stock purchase plan at 20% discount with 2–5 year vesting depending on country of grant	Plans to be reviewed with merger. Plan B well thought out
Expense policy	None	Reimbursement on expense claim	€1000 allowance for sales staff €1500 for allowance management Additional reimbursement on expense claim	Plan B includes a tax-effective allowance which can be transferred easily to Company A. Positive incentive
Travel policy	None	Economy for air travel First class otherwise	Economy for air travel of less than 3 hours Business for longer flights First for other travel	Plan B is more generous than industry standard Transition to Plan A recommended Amount of intercontinental flights are limited
Company car	None	€15–20K for sales staff €40–50K for senior managers	€10K for sales staff €30–45K for VP's	Comparable policy. Plan B cheaper
Luncheon vouchers	None	None but subsidized cafeteria	€150 / month for non-managers	Employees with no access to cafeteria should receive vouchers
Clubs and facilities	None	Free access to Health Club	Free access to Golf and Health Club and company boat	Cost of unifying benefits recommended at hardly any extra cost
Other	None	None	Day care centre for employee's children	Cost is out of proportion compared to benefit. Could be replaced by subsidy Discussion point

Chapter 3

Human Resource Management Information Systems, tools and data transfer action plan

Getting the right pay at the right time after the merger has been completed is a critical satisfaction factor and should not be considered lightly.

Although the IT department will probably take over responsibility for determining in what format data should be transferred from one system to another, it will be your responsibility to determine what data must be transferred in priority – and what data can wait – to ensure smooth processing of salaries. Care should be exercised that, at the time of data transfer, complete control is exercised to ensure that all data remains out of the hands and eyes of unauthorized personnel, and that the right back-ups are made to avoid loss of historic data.

In order not to waste time, and meet the above requirements, the following steps should be followed:

> Step 1: Determine file transfer and field code compatibility between systems

This is generally a team effort between HR and IT. Most modern payroll systems (and HRIS for that matter) include a file-export format facility which permits automation of data transfer from one system to another. However, the order, sequence, length or format of fields may vary from one system to another, requiring a certain amount of testing and manipulation. In any event, a transfer process will need to be established and tested.

> Step 2: Establish common code language

In most European countries (but not in all), there is a strict terminology and date layout and coding for payroll processing. But the same does not apply when extending the process to general personnel information. It is therefore often more effective to split the process (merge payroll first and integrate personnel data later), as the first is pretty much a straightforward procedure. Besides, you may find yourself confronted with branches or subsidiaries having chosen to outsource their payroll, and others that haven't. As a result, you will want to specify service companies able to use the exact terminology and data layout you need, whether you decide to maintain the outsourcing service contract or not.

Step 3: Inform employees of new payment processing system

No matter how thoroughly you proceed with test runs and sample checks, and no matter how well your data transfer lists are prepared, you always run the risk of having forgotten something, or of finding one piece of information that is not being processed correctly. It is a wise move to inform employees when salaries are processed by a new system, and to encourage them to check their payslips carefully to spot any mistakes resulting from the transfer of information.

And once you've completed your preparations, before 'going live', you still need to compare general HR policies and handbooks to complete the review.

Chapter 4

Comparison of general HR policies and handbooks

General HR policies, and the way in which they are presented to new employees are, in many ways, what makes the company distinctive as an employer and comparable in value to an annual report.

Well-written company handbooks are divided into two main parts. The first part is a more general section and provides new employees with insight on the corporation's financial background, international presence, and overall objectives. It will also normally include details such as management style, career opportunities (with success stories), and training and development provision. The second part is a little more like a toolkit; detailing the where's, who's, what's and how's.

You may wonder if the review and eventual replacement of corporate policies and handbooks could not wait until everything else has settled down. For a number of reasons, I believe this topic is just as important (if not more so in some of its indirect implications) as the other issues we have discussed.

a) It is the first piece of formal communication that builds a new corporate identity.
b) It is generally referred to as a supplement to the employment contract and, as such, may include renewed and legally binding commitments until they are changed or cancelled.
c) It may represent the presentation to employees of a general collective labour agreement and as such require labour negotiations and financial commitments before you may change it.
d) It is the logical extension of the compensation and benefit review you have just completed and employees will be expecting detailed feedback on this review. Regardless of point c, the process will probably involve personnel representatives and unions before any implementation. As such, the delivery of a new, commonly agreed upon set of best practice for HR can be a very positive and motivating tool.
e) With the advent of sleek on-line communication tools, you may decide to keep your entire manual on-line, which makes the ever-tedious updating process that much easier.

Finally, corporate handbooks may also include benefits, or miscellaneous issues you overlooked when preparing the global benefit survey *and as such serve as a process check.*

In previous paragraphs, we looked at how to compare benefits. Here, we need to look more closely at 'The mission statement' and 'The policy processes'.

The mission statement

Most employee handbooks contain an introduction by the CEO presenting the company, its lines of business, objectives, culture and values.

In the early process of the acquisition, the communications department generally prepares an information letter to all employees explaining the purpose of the acquisition and what the new company's objectives will be (see Chapter 3 on communication plans). Occasionally it is followed by a reaffirmation of its core values and its HR global strategy.

Most HR mission statements will include commitments such as to:

- Recruit and train staff of the highest quality
- Strive for excellence in providing quality products or services
- Enhance the company's international reputation
- Play a role as a key contributor to the local economy
- Ensure cost-effective management
- Provide state of the art support to employees and management
- Create and maintain a stimulating working environment
- Provide staff with the time and opportunity for leisure, reflection and creativity
- Provide career and personal development opportunities
- Secure the resources needed to achieve personal and corporate goals.

An acquisition process is the ideal time to discuss, with all the partners involved, how to improve your message; to give employees a new sense of purpose and clear indications of the company's objectives.

Some companies have two separate handbooks. The first is often a presentation of the company, describing its core values (and is sometimes used as a corporate brochure too). The second is an employee handbook, which may include excerpts of the first booklet, but focuses mainly on policies, processes and procedures. Some companies will have an all-in-one welcome brochure including both.

The objective of this chapter is not to go into details of how to structure and produce an employee handbook; but we will try to point out, in the process of a merger, how mission statements may differ, how changing the content may impact on employee morale, and what liabilities may result from one or the other.

Issues which may differ and need your particular attention could be statements referring to (but not limited to):

Career and development

Make sure you:

- Compare the stated company's philosophy on promotions and career development. Are there conditions or requirements in one company and not the other? How might this affect the future – and as a result the motivation – of employees of the acquired company?
- Compare statements on training and education, i.e. levels of available sponsorship, retention clauses, etc.
- Compare international career opportunities and postings abroad.

Equal opportunity employment

- Is there a clear mission statement on equal opportunity employment and how is it implemented?
- Is equal opportunity employment a general corporate philosophy, or is it pushed to the point where both sexes must be represented more or less evenly in the different functions of the organization?

Job security

- Are there statements which may be misleading, or leave room for interpretation? Legal advice might be useful here
- Are there conflicting messages referring to job security?

Some typical examples of statements in each of the above categories which can raise an eyebrow include:

Career and development

- *'Promotions to management posts are handled through an assessment and development centre on the basis of senior management's recommendations.'* The implication being that, although the process ensures objective selection, performance alone will not guarantee advancement.
- *'To be eligible for a management position in a specific area, employees must have gained international experience with a subsidiary abroad, as an expatriate, for at least X years.'* This may be explicit, as above, or more subtly implied as follows: *'The opportunity to gain experience in one of our foreign subsidiaries is one of the company's unique personal and career development benefits.'*
- *'The company strongly encourages all employees to adopt a business suit dress code, all managers are required to wear ties; jeans and trainers should be avoided.'* A dress code may sound like a trivial issue, but it is not. The dress code is often part of the company's corporate culture; particularly in an acquisition process where people can be singled out just by the way they dress.

Equal opportunity employment

'In order to ensure equal opportunity employment and career development, the company commits to have at least 40% of men or women represented at each level of management.' What appears as a worthy attempt to address gender issues, may create problems later. This statement may require some form of positive sexual discrimination in the hiring and promotion process – which may come back to haunt you.

Job security

'We pride ourselves in welcoming new employees to our corporate family where they will be treated fairly in a supportive and stimulating environment. Please note however, that all employees of this organization may be terminated with or without cause or notice and are not guaranteed employment for any length of time'. (Source 2001 HR One). Besides giving the wrong message, such statements, although legally acceptable in the US, Switzerland, and, with minor adjustments, the UK, would be totally illegal in most of Western Europe.

As a general recommendation, you will probably find it worth maintaining a very distinct line between the company's mission statement and general commitment to employees, and the employee handbook itself; whether these are two separate documents or combined. Indeed, the first tells you whom you are working for, and the second shows you how.

The policy processes

Beyond the benefits and mission statements themselves, you need to focus on merging of the policy processes, as a priority.

The procedures on expense account approvals, travel organization, sick leave reporting, etc. will undoubtedly vary from one organization to another.

Merging procedures and defining new ones may well not fall into the responsibility of the Human Resources Department. Nevertheless, it is important that you understand the differences in each organization and outline the potential risks for confusion or for establishing underlying and unintended commitments so that HR remains directly involved at various stages of the process.

The form used to compare benefits can also apply here, as illustrated in Table 10.

Table 10 *Comparative benefits process analysis*

Benefit	Request document	Deadlines	Process	Comment
Holidays	A: Holiday request form B: Holiday request form	2 weeks before holiday 4 weeks before holiday	A: Approval of direct superior, and OK from HR B: Direct superior and unit manager and OK from HR	Implement policy of Company B which allows better planning
Illness Accident	Absence form (both companies) or medical certificate	If absence planned (i.e. surgery), as early as possible If unplanned, medical certificate to be forwarded to HR no later than legally prescribed deadline	Supervisor AND HR must be informed on day of illness HR to process claims as defined in loss of salary insurance policy	No change in process needed, but inform employees that both companies have the same loss of salary insurance coverage
Retirement	Early retirement request form. To be requested from HR	A: 6 months before planned retirement B: 6 months before planned retirement	Early retirement is a right. Requires information to unit manager	Same processes
Overtime	A: Overtime sheet B: Based on timesheet	A: End of the month for process during the following month B: No later than 10th of the month for process on same month	A: All overtime exceeding 5 hours in a week needs written request from supervisor and approval from manager B: Superior approves time sheet	A has greater control on overtime. Recommend process of Company A Staff need to be informed
Profit sharing	N/A	N/A	HR communicates premiums on the basis of information received from finance department	None
Stock option plan	Stock option request Stock purchase request Cash in request	A: Stock option grant after trial period and in January of each year Stock purchase anytime within allowed maximum Cash in request one month before cash in (latest) for options, anytime for stock purchased B: Stock option upon commencement date Further requests may be done at any time Stock purchase as Company B	A: Validity of request (vesting period) to be approved by treasury. Payments done by Finance B: Validity of request approved by Finance Payments done through payroll	Process to be reviewed by Finance

Benefit	Request document	Deadlines	Process	Comment
Expense policy	Expense sheet	End of month for process next month A: Provides cash advance of €5000 for managers and €2000 for other eligible staff B: Does not provide cash advances	A: Approval by supervisor. Processed by HR B: Approval by supervisor, checked by Finance, process through HR	Discuss with Finance
Travel policy	Travel request form	A: One day before travel B: Three days before travel	A: Approval from unit manager. Processed through travel agency exclusively B: Approval from unit manager. Employees may organize own travel according to policy	Travel agency will remain, policy of Company A to communicate to all employees
Company car	None	€15–20K for sales staff €40–50K for senior managers	€10K for sales staff €30–45K for VP's	Comparable policy. Plan B cheaper
Lunch vouchers	A: None	Company B distributes €150 vouchers automatically to non-management staff	None	Employees with no access to cafeteria should receive vouchers
Clubs and facilities	A: None B: Request for use of boat	B: First come first served	None	If boat is kept, extend policy to all employees
Other	A: None B: Day care request	None	None	Benefit will probably be suppressed

Note: A refers to Company A. B refers to Company B

Finally, changes in each process, contact person, or nature of benefits must be communicated to staff, ideally through a presentation, followed up in writing.

As mentioned earlier, issuing a Questions and Answers sheet on this, followed by an information newsletter, will save you time and trouble.

In addition to those processes which relate directly to compensation and benefits, Human Resources has a number of other processes of its own, such as:

- Recruitment
- Training
- Promotions
- Terminations.

These need to be reviewed in a similar manner.

In earlier pages, we have seen how to examine mission statements, compensation, benefits, general HR policies, and their relevant procedures; and how to analyse and assess the inherent differences. We have also seen how quickly employees will be asking questions both about how the acquisition will affect their current benefits and what procedures should be followed.

The 'Salary Practice Analysis Table', introduces a summarized action plan.

Consequently, you should have all of the basic ingredients to issue the new policies. One last point. You may want to spend time agreeing:

- The urgency of each policy
- The potential impact change will have on employee morale
- The labour law implications that you need to address before implementing these changes
- How the HR policies reinforce the planned business culture of the merged organizations.

Finally, if you are conducting a pan-European review, you will to need to differentiate clearly between 'corporate' and 'local policies'.

Although the European Union is trying to harmonize basic legal terms of employment, vast disparities still exist, not only in the area of social security, but also in holiday rights, official holidays, company cars, to list but a few.

Tables 11 and 12 are comparisons of such benefits in summary form and are designed for illustrative purposes only.

Table 11 *Typical statutory benefit comparison, by country*

Statutory benefits	Belgium	France	Germany	Italy	UK	Switzerland
Medical care	100% reimbursement by the state for surgical treatment; 65% for doctor's treatment	35%–100% of medical costs reimbursed by the state, if state affiliated doctors are used	Insured persons receive limited hospital and out-patient treatment	All residents are fully covered under National Health Service (SSN)	Full, free coverage by National Health Service. Prescription charge is GBP 5.80	Varies from canton to canton. Most plans provide in/out patient treatment and drugs
Dental care	70%–75% of costs covered by the state	Partially reimbursed	50%–60% reimbursement	Basic treatment provided	–	Basic coverage
Vacation	Employees working a 6 day week are entitled to 24 days leave; for a 5 day week the entitlement is 20 days	Annual vacation is a minimum of 5 weeks, the fifth week must be taken separately from the other four weeks	24 working days based on a 6 day week	4 weeks minimum	EU Working time directive of 4 weeks or collective agreement	4 weeks
Maternity	15 weeks at 82% of salary	16 weeks minimum, with 6 weeks before and 10 weeks after the birth, benefits at 100% of salary minus contributions	Minimum leave is 14 weeks, where 6 weeks are taken before the birth and eight weeks after	Up to 11 months with at least 2 months before birth, where state benefit equals 80% of salary for 5 months, and company is required to top-up to 100%	18 weeks minimum with 22 additional unpaid weeks	Governed by collective agreement and individual work contracts. Benefit equal to full salary, normally for 16 weeks. Varies in some cantons

Table 11   *Typical statutory benefit comparison, by country (continued)*

Statutory benefits	Belgium	France	Germany	Italy	UK	Switzerland
Retirement	Full pension is 60% of adjusted average career earnings, to max BEF1,404,155 For married couples pension is 75%	Full pension is 50% of average earnings over best 14–25 years of employment, to maximum of FRF173,640	Full benefit is 40% of final salary up to the maximum salary ceiling	Pensions will range from a statutory minimum of ITL709,550 per month over a 13 month period	Single pension £66.75, for couples £106.70 per week Earnings related pension 25% of average annual revalued earnings, 20% less for those retiring after April 2000	Annual pension for single person Sfr12,060 to 24,120; married couples 80% of singles (max 150%) + additional pension based on accrued pensioned capital
Retirement age	65	60–65 for both men and women	65	62	65 Men 60 Women	65 Men 62 Women
Contractual termination notice	Claeyes Formula	30 days minimum	4 weeks minimum; for employer increases with years of service	Collective agreement + severance payment = 'Accrued rights' pay	1–12 weeks + 1–2 weeks severance pay per year of service for age 22–40 years	1–3 months
Normal working hours	40 hours / week	35 hours / week	48 hours / week	40 hours	40 hours	40 hours week

Note: A refers to Company A. B refers to Company B

Table 12   Typical benefit comparison for management, by country

Statutory benefits	Belgium	France	Germany	Italy	UK	Switzerland
Medical care	100% reimbursement by the state for surgical treatment; 65% for a doctor's treatment	Provided, dependants covered	Provided	Employers' supplement benefits Dependants are covered	Medical benefit to supplement coverage	Provided, dependants are covered (considered taxable income)
Dental care	Not provided	Provided	As per the statutes	Provided	Not provided	Provided
Insurance	Accident insurance: 70%–80% of annual salary Life Insurance: 24–36 months	Life insurance: dependants covered Accident insurance: 2–3 years' salary	Life insurance: 12 months salary Accident insurance: 24–36 months	Life insurance: 60 months salary Accident insurance: 72 months	Life insurance: 36–48 months salary Accident insurance: 36–48 months	Life insurance: 12–24 months Accident insurance: 24 months
Vacation	21 days after 5 years, 22 days after 10 years	27–30 days	30 days	30 days	25 days	23 days
Maternity	As per the statutes	As per the statutes	As per the statutes	As per the statutes	As per the statutes	16 weeks
Retirement	As per the statutes	As per the statutes	Supplementary plan is based on final salary	As per the statutes	Employer contributes 4–30% and employee 3–8% Pension or lump sum are based on average or final salary	Typical benefit is based on defined contribution Employees typically contribute 6% of annual salary and employer 8–12%
Retirement age	As per the statutes	As per the statutes	As per the statutes	As per the statutes	As per the statutes	As per the statutes
Termination notice	Not provided	As per the statutes + severance payment 12–24 months	As per the statutes + severance payment 3–5 years	As per agreement	By arrangement	As per the statutes
Normal working hours	As per the statutes	As per the statutes	As per the statutes	As per the statutes	As per the statutes	As per the statutes

Source: *Human Resources Atlas*, 2000 edition, William Mercer
Disclaimer: The information provided in this table is a summary of the pertinent local European labour in force in year 2000. It should therefore only be considered as an indication and not as totally reliable reference.

Chapter 5
Designing retention programmes

The quality of your communication process will be a key factor in the success of your retention programme. The turmoil of an acquisition not only triggers fear, loss of purpose and a potential drop in motivation, but it also strains the bonds of loyalty, shared vision and sense of belonging.

Get used to it, these are the arguments head-hunters will use as they attempt to woo your key managers.

As the threat of losing good people increases, so does the problem of replacing them: outside candidates are often reluctant to join a company going through upheaval; and internal applicants – if there are any – are usually sorely needed where they are, and cannot move to new departments.

There are four key ingredients to professional job satisfaction:

1. Job stability.
2. New and rewarding responsibilities.
3. Future prospects.
4. Job recognition.

It is these four elements that will be discussed in this chapter. We will go through the steps to help retain key players in the different stages of the process, nurture confidence and strengthen a feeling of belonging.

There are two main types of retention programme:

1. Programmes to retain key players during the integration process.
2. Programmes to retain employees in the new organization.

Although not necessarily unconnected, these two types of programme have different objectives and duration. The first is designed to secure a small group of people on a short-term basis; people whose leadership skills, ability to mobilize the troops, and, in particular, special knowledge of products, processes or technology, are vital in the early stages of integration.

The second is a longer-term process to keep good people motivated, focused on business goals, and boosted by a feeling of belonging, and of being part of the integration process.

Programmes to retain key players during the integration process

---

Step 1: Identify your key players

The whole of your management team are not necessarily key players in the integration process. The real key players are more likely to be a handful of senior executives or line managers who possess *knowledge* without which the speed, effectiveness, or even success of the preliminary integration could be jeopardized. The same may also apply to a few of their direct reports or even employees with highly specific skills.

You may feel that senior executives have, if not a binding obligation to 'stick it through' at the very least a moral commitment to support the process. You may also argue that some local European labour legislation (such as in Switzerland, for example) expressly forbids ill-timed resignations. No matter how valid that argument may be in theory, practice often proves it worthless, with dire consequences. Bearing in mind what may be at stake, is the possibility of losing key players worth the risk?

The Chief Financial Officer, Technical Director, Legal Adviser, HR Director and senior executives in Product Development, Sales (and if you are a manufacturing company, R&D, Manufacturing, Procurement and Distribution) of *both* companies are generally considered key players in the early stages of integration. The same does not necessarily apply so obviously to managers in Marketing, Retail, Administration and Support and Communications.

The position will obviously vary from one organization to another. Nor does it necessarily follow that ALL key players must be placed on retention programmes. The decision of who is a key player and which of these to place on a retention programme is the choice of the CEO.

Step 2: Define the retention package

Retention packages are meant to last only through the first phase of the integration, which is generally a short period of perhaps 3–6 months.

Often referred to as 'golden handcuffs', they represent a financial advantage, which is paid out at the end of the retention period. As they should represent a strong measure of recognition, communicating them properly is extremely important.

Below is a copy of a retention letter, which was sent by a company to the key managers of a firm they acquired in 2001. As you will see, it starts well but then continues less successfully.

Dear ...
   You are aware that ABC Inc. is in the process of acquiring XYZ. This process will involve extensive changes to the business. The acquisition is a crucial stage in the development of ABC Inc. and it is vital that we have the right people in place to enable us to hit our targets and achieve our strategic goals.
   We have identified you as a key person in the successful integration of XYZ Company and ABC Inc. Before the acquisition takes place we will be assessing the needs of the combined businesses going forward and would like you to be part of that assessment process.
   We know that these may be uncertain times for you but are very keen that you remain with XYZ and assist us with this process of rapid assessment, change and development.

This is a good introduction as it contains the right emotionally charged messages:

- *'We have identified **you** as a key person ...' It is a personal note, more effective than 'We have identified a number of key players ...', as it gives the manager a true sense of self worth.*
- *'We are very keen that you remain with the company [...] in this process of rapid assessment, change and development'. This a stabilizing message, indicating that the manager is not only needed within the organization, but that his opinion will be valued at strategic level.*

The letter then proceeded as follows:

   In order to confirm our commitment to this process and to your assistance with the integration of the two businesses, you will receive an ex gratia payment of 20% of your annual salary (in addition to your other contractual payments) provided you remain with the merged business until [date]. This is the date by which we hope that the integration process should be complete.

Comment: This sentence, which was meant to give a clear indication of the financial reward, and be a motivational factor actually opened a can of worms.
   The recipients interpreted 'annual salary' as 'annual gross compensation – i.e. including bonus' whereas ABC Inc meant 'annual base salary'. The financial impact of extending the percentage to annual gross

compensation would have been minimal and immediately closed the subject, but ABC Inc. decided against it. As a result, and even though the package was considered generous (and that most managers concerned didn't even expect a retention bonus) this confusion was an unfortunate start. It led to a climate of mistrust and demonstrated an unfortunate lack of attention for detail.

> As we have not yet carried out the assessment process to determine what is required to take business forward, it is difficult to confirm that there will be a job for you at the end of the process. However, if it is the case that there will not be a job for you at the end of the assessment period, we will make any legal and contractual payments to you in the usual way, in addition to the ex gratia payment referred to above.
> [...]
> We have adopted this approach because whilst all employees may be at risk of redundancy, we see you as a vital member of the team through this time of change and are anxious to encourage you to remain with the business to assist us with this venture.

Comment: This is undoubtedly one of the worst ways to introduce a retention package, and this is how it was received:

- *'We haven't determined what is required to take the business forward', in other words: 'we haven't done our homework, neither do we know what our business requirements will be nor whom we will need to meet them. In fact, we're not quite sure of what we're doing, but we're playing it safe.'*
- *In total contradiction to our comments in the first and subsequent paragraph that you are a key player in the organization, please consider that you may not be key in the future. Please give us all you can during the integration process but remain prepared to be made redundant, regardless of how successfully you complete what we request of you.*
- *We are clearly required to make contractual payments to you but as no mention is made about severance pay, we may be debating whether this is a retention bonus or some sort of pre-termination package.*
- *'Whilst all employees may be at risk of redundancy, we see you as a vital member of the team ...' In other words: 'we may have to terminate vital members of the team such as you, but expect you to remain focused on the business throughout the process.'*

Needless to say, these subsequent paragraphs destroyed any beneficial effects the retention programme may have had. As a result, most managers who received the letter started eagerly looking for new jobs, trying to time their resignations with the retention deadlines in order to get the full financial benefits and secure their future at the same time.

In fact, some managers who had not found other jobs at the end of the retention period had been so upset by the approach (and, in all fairness, to other similar issues of which this was just one example) that they requested to be made redundant and receive a severance package, rather than to have to endure further undermining of their confidence.

The letter concluded:

> If this is acceptable to you, we would be grateful if you would sign and return the enclosed copy [. . .] indicating your acceptance of our invitation to remain with the Company until [date].

This paragraph raises unnecessary questions:

- *'If this is acceptable to you …' does this mean we can negotiate?*
- *If I don't sign it, will it be considered as a resignation?*
- *If I sign it and resign before the end of retention date, are their penalties involved, beyond not receiving the ex gratia payment?*

A retention package is a commitment by the company to its key people. It is not a mutual agreement. *It specifies when it starts, when it ends, and the financial reward at a given date. If penalties are to be attached, or if financial rewards are based on (measurable) individual performance, then it is no longer a retention package and simply represents special terms of employment over a given period of time. The two may ultimately have the same purpose, but legally they are quite different documents and need to be handled differently.*

There are three golden rules to remember when devising retention packages:

1. Limit your retention letter to a single key message: 'You are key to the integration process'. The commitment of the company does not go beyond that statement and there is no benefit to be had in reminding people of that fact. The retention letter should be a warm and motivating note, focusing on the importance of the individual to the process. It should not be spoiled by other considerations. Although the reward itself is an important part of the retention strategy, the simple fact that you have been identified and valued as a key strategic player is likely to have the greatest impact.
2. Make sure you are clear how the rewards are defined and *leave no room for interpretation*. If the reward is a lump sum, make it clear whether the amount will be paid in local currency equivalent (at a given date) or in another specified currency. If it is a percentage of salary, define the term *salary*. If it is

a benefit, make sure you explain the benefit in full. For example: if you offer a company car, don't forget to specify if it will be run under the terms of the company scheme, and whether costs such as petrol, insurance, and so on are to be borne by the beneficiary.

3. Remember that a retention letter rewards, first and foremost, loyalty. If you want to include a bonus based on successful completion of a project within a given deadline, this involves a different approach. If this is the case, prepare two separate documents. The first one being the retention letter with an ex gratia payment at a given date (and which does not require mutual agreement), and a second one, which is a specific performance related bonus, and where terms and conditions must be jointly defined and agreed by both the individual and the company.

Although you may save yourself some effort by the use of a global catch-all approach to the retention strategy (same package for all involved), there is no reason not to have a specific package for specific people. ABC Inc. for example paid its managers a 20 per cent bonus if they stayed until September 29th, and a 30 per cent bonus if they remained with the company until December 31st. Naturally, some of the managers calculated that it made more sense to stay until the end of September, and consequently those who stayed for the extra 10 per cent felt they had to work longer for proportionally less.

Direct cash compensation[1] is the most common form of retention package. However, there are many other ways to reward loyalty. For example:

1. Predetermined lump sums
2. Tax effective contribution to the individual's pension fund or capitalized life insurance
3. Stock ownership in the new combined entity
4. A period of fully paid vacation for employee and family in a plush resort
5. One year tuition for dependant child(ren) in private schools
6. Sponsorship – one employee at XYZ had their yacht sponsored for an important race, rather than receive the money directly
7. Heavily discounted or free ownership of corporate assets (portable computers, company cars, furniture, art works, even real-estate).[2]

Once you have:

• Identified your key players
• Determined the packages, and
• Prepared the letters (and have them checked by your legal adviser and if possible, re-read by a neutral person).

You must:

1 Remember to specify if the direct cash compensation will be subject to national insurance and income tax.
2 This can be an interesting approach as such items are often fully amortized in the company accounts and hence offer a corporate tax break.

Step 3: Communicate and implement the programme

In the example above, all that happened was that the letter was sent out. That was it. Had it been properly drafted, it would still have raised a couple of questions (should I call and thank my CEO? Who are the other key players? What happens next?). It also missed the opportunity not only to give the key executives a personal word of thanks and encouragement, but also to invite their immediate questions and concerns.

At such a crucial moment in the integration, a piece of welcome news such as a retention package should be exploited to the maximum. For example, you might:

- Organize a meeting with all involved (even if it means flying them in from their current locations)
- If possible, hold the meeting outside office premises
- Have a presentation ready about the current status of the integration
- Tell them why they have been invited, what is expected of them, and what is in their retention packages[3]
- Hold a *short* Q&A session, and since this moment is worth celebrating, celebrate it!

As a last reminder:

- Make sure payroll receives a copy of the packages. I have often witnessed examples where this has been inadvertently overlooked, or where it was taken for granted that it would be the employees themselves who would forward their letter to the Personnel department!
- Finally, when time comes for the payment of the pro gratia bonus, make sure you follow it up with a thank you note, or if appropriate hold another update meeting.

Programmes to retain employees in the new organization

These programms are longer-term than the retention plans for key managers and specialists. They apply to all staff, regardless of rank and competence. They give meaning to the expression: 'Our strength is our people, and we care about them'. The success of such programmes is much more dependent on the leadership and communication skills of those handling the deal than on the financial rewards on offer.

Most companies already have a retention or employee satisfaction programme of some sort. Although the quality of their implementation may vary considerably

---

3 If you have specific packages for specific people, you don't need to go into individual details, but simply mention that the company wants to express their appreciation for their loyalty as indicated in the letters you will be giving them shortly.

from one organization to another, the structure of these plans is generally quite similar, and include:

- Learning and development opportunities
- Training and career development programmes
- Stock ownership and similar benefits
- Newsletters and employee information processes.

Following a merger or acquisition, at a time when everything is being scrutinized and assessed and, where career opportunities appear to be at risk, it may take a little more to keep employees motivated.

Try the following steps:

Step 1: Welcome

You may remember that in the chapter on communication, the timing and contents of a 'welcome to our company' note were discussed, as well as how to brief managers and help them to communicate the deal to their staff.

Whether or not your company is planning redundancies in the near future as a result of the acquisition, there will be a transition period during which all employees will be in the same boat. This period is often one of high anxiety, frustration and doubt. As a result, this first welcome message should focus on:

- The rationale for the deal
- The mission and strategy of the combined organization
- The confidence the companies have in the ability of their people to join forces and lead a successful integration process.

This welcome message should be shortly followed by a general get-together.

Step 2: Socialize

In most cases, employees of each company are unlikely to know each other. Groups tend to form around members of 'Company A' versus 'Company B'. Employees may even hesitate to mingle with those of the other organization, fearing that their colleagues – or worse, managers – might disapprove or even consider it disloyal.

It is essential to give all employees the opportunity and the encouragement to get acquainted with each other, share their visions and hopes, and start laying the first plans for future combined teams.

Until the deal is done, however, double check with legal advisers that this approach is acceptable as it may not be if you are a publicly traded company with a longer shareholder acceptance period. In which case both companies may technically remain competitors until the deal has been ratified. You may want to socialize but you must remain at arm's length. If this is the case, communicate with your people and let them know the score.

Planning for the first social meeting between the two workforces should start early after the announcement, and may require some thought:

- You may want to brief your local managers on the topics to be stressed, and others which are not yet up for comment or discussion
- Next, you may have to decide between a global, general meeting and locally organized events, or a combination of both
- Thirdly, you will probably need to establish a budget and suggest a general style for the meeting in order to ensure consistency in the approach
- Finally, you may choose to communicate the next steps of the integration process during these events.

A well-organized meeting will undoubtedly increase the chances of positive cooperation and goodwill between the people involved. When the time comes to set up groups who will work together on further integration issues, you will probably find that the original resistance or resentment that prevailed prior to such meetings has been replaced by goodwill from both parties.

Step 3: Involve

Involvement of the workforce is critical. By now teams should have been set up to review and assess the way the different departments and divisions of the company operate, but the members of such teams only represent a fraction of the workforce. In order to keep up momentum, feedback, and a general feeling of purpose from employees in each company, you need to make them feel they are an integral part of the deal and that their contributions are valued.

- Make sure all employees know who the integration team-leaders are and how they can be contacted
- Take the time to listen. People need to talk about what they consider important, to important people. By having, if not daily at least weekly, slots in your agenda for one-on-one meetings, you will not only manage to provide people with the warm messages they need, but often defuse potential conflicts
- Encourage everyone (through memos, newsletters, intranet, etc.) to share ideas, make suggestions or voice concerns. Provide them with the tools to do so (suggestion box, e-mail, meetings, etc.). Do not forget to guarantee *and respect their anonymity* if they so desire
- Make sure your integration managers are properly coached to handle these messages and provide regular feedback and recognition to those providing them.

This last point is particularly important, and although it may require, in some instances, more time and attention that the topic itself would normally deserve, its payback is well worth the effort.

Step 4: Engage

Times of change are not only times of uncertainty but also times of opportunity. The way these opportunities are communicated will play a significant role in your employees' readiness to 'stick it through'.

Your communication manager will be one of the key players in finding the tone, tools and timing to keep employees engaged and committed, but most of the responsibility will be yours.

The following are some examples of what you can do:

1. New employment opportunities and vacancies should be *widely* publicized during the integration, particularly at a time when hiring freezes are usually the norm. Encourage employees even more so than usual, to introduce friends and relations as possible candidates.
2. Whenever possible, open the vacancies in other countries, which would normally be restricted to locals only, to all employees. You will need to consider the cost of relocation, but what you will gain in retention of knowledge, loyalty and morale should far outweigh the cost of such programmes, which can be easily halted after completion of the integration.
3. Provide new training and learning facilities in line with the acquisition. Get professional trainers to work alongside your managers and provide top-notch presentations and workshops.
4. Keep people focused on business goals and organize sales/production contests, and get the back-office people involved as well. Don't forget to communicate the successes.
5. Set-up a help desk or facilitation programmes where either in-house or external consultants can help employees manage through the change.
6. Revamp your website and intranet and invite all to contribute to the new design, layout and even content.
7. Consider putting the services of a career counsellor or work psychologist at the disposal of employees to help manage through the change.

In short, during an acquisition, you are at risk not only of losing key people, but also of finding it difficult to recruit candidates willing to join a company.

Even before you conduct assessments to help identify the organization's future players, you must select and secure – at least for the life span of the process – those people whose knowledge and skills are paramount to the success of the integration. Success in retaining these people will depend almost exclusively on your strategy for involving and rewarding everyone.

At a time of insecurity, the need for recognition, reassurance and involvement is at its peak. Although new compensation and benefit strategies will definitely play a role in retaining employees in the long run, the immediate priority is to:

- Welcome the players in the new organization
- Integrate teams and involve them in the process
- Regularly unveil new challenges and opportunities.

Regular communication and coaching will help you limit substantially the risks of high employee turnover.

Summary

In order to ensure seamless integration of employees, you need to gain a thorough understanding of the terms of employment and compensation and benefits. Take time for a thorough analysis of:

- Employment contracts
- Salaries, commissions and other forms of financial rewards
- Insurance policies
- Other cash and non-cash benefits.

Identification with loyalty to an employer is also linked to the company's global policies and mission statement. Make sure the following all deliver an appropriate message:

- Corporate handbooks
- Career and development policies
- Training and learning opportunities.

Finally, in troubled times, special attention should be given to retention and incentive programmes to keep staff motivated and committed to the success of the merger.

Part III

The integration stage

I'm slowly becoming a convert to the principle that you can't motivate people to do things, you can only de-motivate them. The primary role of a manager is not to empower but to remove obstacles.

Scott Adams

In this section you will learn how to:

- Make sure the companies use similar processes and have a shared vocabulary to describe them
- Establish manpower plans
- Conduct organization and assessment programmes
- Review local labour laws
- Prepare and conduct terminations
- Finalize transfers and integration

Chapter 1

Process review

In Part I, Chapter 3, Figure 1, the sample organization chart of the integration team, illustrated a Product and Sales unit and showed the relationship of the unit to the organisation's Sales Director.

Arguably, Sales should stick to sales integration, Human Resources to HR integration and so on, during the integration – the value of an HR representative getting involved in the sales process may seem questionable.

Although there are several ways to integrate teams and their respective compensation and benefit systems, the following approach offers a significant advantage. It allows you to identify the HR implications (including workforce integration, manpower planning and in particular commission and sales-bonus systems) alongside the compensation and benefit comparison. As a result, any potential areas of concern may be spotted and comprehended in such a way to allow for timely corrective measures.

Review of products and sales

The steps outlined below relate to HR and are of course only a fraction of what *the sales integration team* will be looking at. However, they are necessary for the HR aspects of the integration because of their direct impact on people.

Step 1: Compare products and sales approach

The first step involves a full understanding of the sales process in both organizations. This will require a flow chart detailing the different steps and interdependencies of the process.

As a second step, you need to gain a good idea of the product strategy that will emerge from this integration. Ask yourself:

- Which of the two product sets are complementary?
- Which products will be retained?
- Which products will be discontinued?
- Will a new product family arise to better meet customer/client expectations?

Take time to explore how sales will be supported by IT. What impact will the acquisition have on merging both companies' technologies? How will sales and services be invoiced and booked, from an accounting perspective?

Sketch the first outline of what the combined sales organization should look like and how it affects current reporting lines.

Step 2: Identify HR implications

Once you understand the sales process(es), you will be able to identify the first areas of potential overlap. These may include duplication of functions, overlapping of territories, or potential overstaffing. It may also reveal weaknesses in resourcing and competences. All of the above will prove a valuable head start when assessing manpower requirements, training needs and potential redundancies.

Creating an overview of the product mix and the sales and marketing strategies will prove essential when it comes to analysing the commission and bonus systems, defining transitional and final compensation strategies, as well as determining sales objectives.

An understanding of how the back-office and IT functions support the sales process lays the groundwork for job definition and job descriptions, levels of responsibilities and overall autonomy, as well as giving you insight into the complexities of processes such as accounting, IT, budgeting, invoicing, and commissioning.

The first outline sketch of the new sales organization will confirm or refute only preliminary conclusions and help to take corrective action before the first steps are taken.

It will also help identify the best practices and the process changes that are needed. Don't take it for granted that the acquiring company must have, by definition, the best processes and tools. By exploring each company's way of doing things, and trying to integrate the best of both worlds into the new organization, you will not only improve the global team spirit, cohesion and integration of the working groups themselves, but most probably identify techniques, products and methodologies better designed to meet client needs.

In summary, a review of the set up of the sales process and product development will give you a preliminary picture of possible conflict areas; potential redundancies; succession and transition issues; immediate and future training and development needs; compensation and commission system problems and so on.

Step 3: Review preliminary findings with the relevant integration manager

---

During an integration process, managers are often involved in so many meetings, workshops and other discussion groups, that they find it very tempting to try to skip joint reviews of preliminary findings.

Of course, you may come up with great ideas and projects of your own, but in HR, you are ultimately dealing with the teams of other managers, and no matter how good your ideas are, you stand a solid chance of being seriously challenged by senior colleagues if you propose, without warning, alternatives to their levels of responsibility, manpower budgets, compensation systems or management scope. In a period as sensitive as this one, you should carefully review such an approach.

Keep in mind that this is still a preliminary review, designed to help you and the manager involved set the basis for the final integration. Consequently, you will be discussing pure approach strategies rather than the detail of how to implement them at this stage of the process.

These will include:

- Job description and responsibility issues:
  - Do both companies use comparable terminology to describe their functions, reporting and responsibility levels, and if not, what is needed to establish comparative tables?

- Compensation and commission systems:
  - How does compensation compare – at first sight – between both groups?
  - How should the commission systems be reviewed?
  - What plans do you have for salary and commissions during the transition period?

- Duplication/suppression of tasks:
  - What positions have duplicates and require assessments to select the best employee?
  - What positions will probably be suppressed? Are there alternatives for the people involved?

- Training and support issues:
  - Are there immediate training needs to ensure the smooth transition of product knowledge?
  - Are facilitators needed to coach teams and prepare employees to accept and buy into the future vision?

Finally, remember that at this stage, you are only sharing preliminary concerns and findings. Although the Sales/Product Integration Manager will of course play a key role in the different stages mentioned above, HR must retain full and final responsibility in the design or approval, implementation and communication of such plans.

Review of the vocabulary used for job descriptions and responsibilities

You need to obtain a clear understanding of each company's *modus operandi* if you want to be in a position to conduct proper personnel assessments which will help you identify and select the company's future personnel, compare compensation and benefits, design an attractive plan, and finally propose a new organizational and reporting structure.

It may be that one or both companies already have an internal grading system such as those designed by Hay, Mercer, Whatson Wyatt and so on. If this is the case, all you need to do is prepare a sheet comparing terminology and grading for both companies (similar to the one shown later in this chapter).

However, if no data of this type is readily available, depending on your needs and the time at hand, you may wish to use external consultants to perform a detailed comparative 'x-ray' of job equivalencies between both organizations, or to do it yourself. A few simple steps and principles will provide you with the basic information you need to move forward. These include:

1. Identify the groups for comparison
2. Define the basic weighting criteria
3. List job titles and their equivalents
4. Prepare a comparison sample.

Identify the groups for comparison

This involves preparing a common method of coding different employee categories. For example:

- Sales or other direct revenue generating functions
- Administrative support functions (Finance, HR, Marketing, Security)
- Technical support (IT, Production)
- Other functions.

Define the basic weighting criteria

Weighting techniques vary widely from company to company. Some use points, others use alpha-numeric systems, and others may use general terminology.

The system I favour is a matrix, which examines two interdependencies. First, the employee's autonomy for decision-making (does he or she need clearance/ checking from superiors for important transactions?) Second, how damaging will a poor decision/underperformance be? Might it have immediate effect on share price, treasury or liquidity, assets, corporate versus local bottom line, reputation, and so on?

It is easy to use, can be applied throughout the organization or tailor-made for a department, and can then be attached to any algorithm or point system you like. Table 1 offers an example of the system.

Table 1 depicts a 4 × 8 criteria matrix. Of course, you can tailor it, rendering it more or less complex or detailed, and set up your own measurement scale. The example is a broad and general management evaluation table. You could also design it specifically for sales and revenue where the impact would go from 'no financial incidence' to 'determines company's viability', and the responsibilities from 'support sales effort' to 'establishes global strategy and budgets, and monitors team to achieve them'.

The points can be further weighted by hierarchical level and/or supervisory role. For example, a company with five levels of hierarchy could have:

General Manager   = 1.2
Sr Vice-President = 1.175
Vice-President   = 1.15
Manager   = 1.125
Deputy   = 1.1

And also the size of the department managed. For example:

1–3   direct reports = 1.1
3–10   direct reports = 1.2
10–20 direct reports = 1.3
20–50 direct reports = 1.4
> 50   direct reports = 1.5

To illustrate this, let's take three examples:

First example: Sales Director Europe, reporting to the Chief Operating Officer, and in charge of 12 area sales managers (each one responsible for their own teams). In the matrix, the Sales Director would probably correspond to line 7: 'Ensures complex tasks requiring superior skills, knowledge and management abilities'. And column c: 'Errors may cause serious delays, extra costs, and loss of revenue or client dissatisfaction, which will have a direct impact on reputation, production or profits', representing an initial score of 33.

Since the Director reports to the COO, who in turn reports to the CEO, they are third in the reporting layers giving them a weighting of 1.15 or a subsequent score of 37.95 (33 × 1.15).

Supervising a team of 12, their supervisor rating is 1.3, giving them a final score of 49.335 (49 rounded).

As a second example, let us imagine the Sr Vice-President Marketing, reporting directly to the CEO, and managing a team of six direct reports. Their score could be imagined as: 45 × 1.175 × 1.2 = 63.

As a third example, the corporate IT Director, reporting to the CFO and having eight direct reports, could read: 37 × 1.15 × 1.2 = 51.

Finally, most salary surveys include short job descriptions and points attached to each which you can also use as a shortcut when preparing the comparison chart.

Table 1   Example of a criteria matrix for weighting candidates

	a). Impact of errors will be limited to work and will have no, or hardly any effect on the course of business	b). Impact of errors may create delays or costs but without seriously affecting the course of business	c). Errors may cause serious delays, extra costs, and loss of revenue or client dissatis-faction, which will have a direct impact on reputation, production or profits	d). Errors could seriously damage the company's reputation, productivity, treasury, and overall revenues; or create serious liabilities
1. Executes work given by superior	1	9	14	20
2. Does mainly execution work but may decide on minor changes or timings	2	10	16	23
3. Does some execution work, but takes own decisions in the execution process. Has limited delegation authority	4	11	19	27
4. Works autonomously on the basis of specific guidelines. May delegate simple execution work	6	13	22	31
5. Works autonomously on the basis of general guidelines. May delegate execution work	8	15	25	35
6. Ensures some complex tasks, involving several parameters and requiring autonomy and initiative	12	18	29	40
7. Ensures complex tasks requiring superior skills, knowledge and management abilities	14	21	33	45
8. Ensures very complex tasks requiring superior skills, vision, and strategic ability	16	24	37	50

One of the main values of this sort of tool during the integration process is that it helps identify differences in professional level, regardless of titles or denominations used. See Box 1.

Box 1: Responsible or accountable?

In service Company A, each Country Managing Director had full bottom line responsibility for sales and revenue in his territory, whereas their counterpart in Company B, although accountable for the well running of the business in general, does not have operational responsibility for sales in particular.

In Company B, the sales function reports to a European Sales Director who in turn reports directly to the US (bypassing the CEO Europe). The importance of this 'exception' is not apparent from the job descriptions, but is quickly revealed in the matrix. Differences in professional requirements, for apparently similar positions in the two organizations, are much wider than originally perceived. Local reporting lines, responsibility for budgeting of sales, and more globally, the design of the European organization itself needs rethinking.

Without totally revolutionizing the corporate structure, this brings a new approach to the way leadership and assessments of local management (and the sales forces) need to be evaluated during the integration process. Ultimately, it will be a determining factor in the selection process to define the right profiles for executives in the new company, which in turn will have a trickle down impact on job descriptions, training needs, and management skills.

List job titles and their equivalents

The logical next step – list and compare job titles – is a simple and straightforward exercise, but an extremely important one. First, you need to establish what titles the different companies use and how they compare (see Table 2 and Table 3).

Table 2   *Job titles*

Company A	Company B
General Manager	Managing Director
Senior Vice-President	Senior Manager
Manager	Head of ...
Head of ...	Supervisor
Receptionist	Director of First Impressions*

* This is actually what appears on the business card of a receptionist in London!

Table 3   *Terminology*

Company A	Company B
Controller	Head of Finance
Web Designer	Internet Art Director
After sales	Client Relationship
Human Resources	Personnel
Life insurance broker	Investment counsellor

Second, what functional terminology is used and how do they compare?

You can then determine, not only what common terminology to use during the process (which will later also govern comparisons, further assessments, leadership requirements, etc.), but also highlight early, potential areas of concern such as: titles to be used, impact on reporting, impact on compensation and commission structures, and so on.

Prepare a comparison sample

Finally, and as a compiled document, you need to establish a comparative list summarizing department terminology, titles, levels and compensation, in order to help you prepare a preliminary recommendation plan. Such a comparison sample might look like Table 4.

By now you have analysed a number of differences in the way the two companies work, established similarities and synergies as well as duplications or redundant tasks. This gives you the base elements to start reviewing with the other integration managers as part of your preliminary sketching of the new company's organization chart, reporting and manpower needs.

Table 4   Comparison of job titles, terms and vocabulary used

	Company A	Company B	Concern	Plan
Title	V.P. Sales	Sales Director	In view of territory split and the size of accounts, Sales Director would be a Key Account Manager in Company A	Acquisition plan to increase market share by 20%. Assess opportunity to have 2 V.P. sales and the potential for the Sales Director to take that role. Need to redesign global sales organization
Department	Int'l Sales	Int'l Sales	None	
Weighting	40	38	None	
Salary range	130–150K	100–110K	None	
Bonus	25%	20%	Commission system is different	Review commission system with V.P. Sales & COO
Value of benefits	20K	10K		
Title	Telesales Manager	Sales Call Centre Supervisor		
Department	Int'l Sales	Country Sales	Different sales organization	Review sales organization
Weighting	16	15		
Salary range	Commission based Perf. Based	Base + Commission Perf. Based	Compensation	Review sales compensation system
Bonus	5K	0	Company car policy	
Value of benefits				
Title	Director IT	IT Manager	Duplicate function	Assess redundancies according to conclusions of assessment centre, length of service and performance appraisals
Department	IT	Finance	CFO will probably need to relinquish IT responsibility	Organize round table with those concerned
Weighting	42	42	None	
Salary range	100–110K	110–120K	None	
Bonus	10K	15%	Depending on final choice, may require change of contractual terms of employment	
Value of benefits	10K	0		
Title	Content Manager	Web Designer	In Company B, content is defined in business and development and not in IT. The Web designer has an execution role. In Company A, Content Manager does both	Discuss with IT further needs and assess competence pool
Department	IT	IT (in Finance)		
Weighting	26	20		
Salary range	70–90K	65–80K	Company B pays over market standard	
Bonus	0	0		
Value of benefits	10K	0		
Title	Controller	Finance Manager	Title to be reviewed	To integrate in the global title review
Department	Finance	Finance		
Weighting	27	42		
Salary range	80–90K	60–70K	Although size of unit is smaller in Company B, responsibilities and qualifications are similar. Salary may need review	Keep in mind during Compensation and Benefits review
Bonus	No bonus	No bonus		

Chapter 2

Manpower planning, assessments and redundancies

One of the most crucial parts of any M&A process involves identifying who will be part of the new organization and who will not.

Unfortunately there is no perfect way of handling a process which unavoidably leads some people to lose their jobs or see their responsibilities reshuffled. However, there are a few rules that can ease the way to a smoother transition. Some of these rules were covered briefly in Chapter 3 of Part I on communication, but the following now deserve closer consideration:

1. Ensure that the process is transparent
2. Provide regular, complete and to the point communication
3. Define manpower needs.

Transparency of the process

There is nothing worse in an M&A process than to leave doubt in employees' minds on how the reorganization process will take place. Employees know that changes will affect jobs, responsibilities and reporting. Denying them the right to have a clear view of how and when that process will take place, on the basis that it might create unwanted turmoil or insecurity is a wrong approach.

You already have unwanted turmoil and insecurity. Keeping people unaware, or letting them have glimpses of what may be in store during the next few months, will only increase their anxiety and lead to ugly rumours.

Explaining how a process will work does not mean you need to reveal all of the sensitive strategies that top management may have in mind. It means describing the method that will be used to define the best organization, with a fair and equitable approach. Presenting the process in an open and direct manner will often trigger constructive questions which will not only help you improve it, but often enable you to gain support in implementing it.

Regular and complete communication

Your communication manager should prepare a communication agenda which is in line with the process explained to staff.

At each step of the process, a short information note should be issued, briefing them on the completion of that step and offering general comments relating to both it and the beginning of the next. Each of these notes should include a contact name for further information. Below is a sample letter illustrating these points:

Dear _____

As you may have read in the press release we issued this morning, ABC International has concluded a strategic negotiation about the future of the company which involves a merger with XYZ. Let me outline the basis for the merger and to explain how it will affect you over the next few weeks and months.

Whilst the merger with XYZ will secure the future of our company and enable us to improve our competitiveness across the global market, our recent poor performance and the continuing weakness of the world economy means that we need to take some pre-emptive steps to ensure the financial viability of the combined company over the short and medium term.

As a result, we will start a manpower planning process next week which we expect to lead to a 25% reduction in our workforce worldwide. We will be making the majority of the reductions in back office and administrative roles. Employees in some countries will be more affected than in others.

In order to ensure the process is fair, we will undertake an independent assessment of all employees, including all administrative, management and professional staff. This will allow us to establish the appropriate levels of staff for the new joint organization. We have retained professional consultants to run the process. They will ensure an objective assessment of the skills and competencies we need as a business and identify the right people for the right jobs. This will be an opportunity to identify individual development needs too and make sure we support these as we go forward.

The process will begin immediately and will adhere to the employment law requirements in each country concerned. We are developing a transitional employee assistance programme for those employees selected for redundancy. The programme will provide resources to support them and help them locate other employment, appropriate to their talent and skills, as quickly as possible.

I firmly believe that our inherent strength is our people. Were this not the case, we would never have achieved the levels of growth that have been possible in the past. All of which makes this an extremely difficult announcement and we have been careful to approach the process with concern and respect for all our employees.

> We will remain in contact with you throughout the period of the merger. However, your normal lines of communication are also open. If you have questions that we have not addressed or that you feel more comfortable discussing with your line manager, please do so.
> You may also contact the following people for more information ...

You may adopt a different style or language but, in essence, this letter covers most key issues at the time it is circulated:

• What is expected from the merger?	Increased competitiveness in a global market
• What is the current situation?	Current and continuing poor performance
• What steps are being taken?	Reduction in the number of employees, particularly in back office and administrative staff
• How and who will handle the process?	An independent assessment of all employees by external consultants
• When will the process start?	Immediately
• What will happen to those affected?	They will be offered a transitional employee assistance programme to help them find other employment
• Where can you get further information?	From your line manager or other (nominated) managers.

Although the shock of knowing that the company will proceed with a 25 per cent staff reduction remains strong, its impact is funnelled in such a way as to inform those who may be affected (rather than alarming the entire staff) and also to reassure that group of employees that assistance and support will be provided – thus easing the trauma caused by such an announcement.

Definition of manpower needs

An effective manpower plan includes both qualitative and quantitative considerations. It needs to consider the organization itself, the jobs, the headcount and the assignment of individuals to specific positions.

Or, in other words, it will include:

• *Organizational forecasting: what will the new organization look like?*
Normally, a sketch of the new combined organization should have been drawn out, if not before the Due Diligence process, at least shortly after. If you don't already have an outline it's high time you address the issue.

- *Qualitative forecasting: what skills will we need (short and longer term)?*
  It is essential to define at an early stage what skills will be required, and how these requirements may evolve in the near future. This process also sheds light on skills, training needs and potential personnel turnover.
- *Quantitative forecasting: what headcount do we need?*
  This is of course the core issue which integrates business objectives with human resources and will ultimately lead to your detailed manpower plan.
- *Individual forecasting: with whom will we be working?*
  Undoubtedly the most delicate and often the most emotional part of the plan, it requires the assessment of individual competencies and leadership skills.

The above can be illustrated as in Figure 1.

You need to translate your plan onto paper and take into account a number of variables and areas of concern.

Tables 5, 6 and 7 are based on the merger of two organizations in the Services sector and employing respectively, at the time of the merger, 600 employees for the first and 400 for the second.

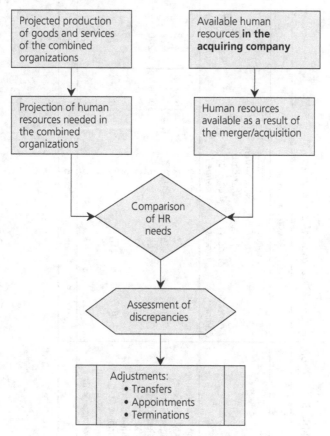

Figure 1   Human Resources forecasting process flow chart

Table 5 *Projected combined available resources*

	Company A				Company B				*Total projected available resources*
Category	*Headcount Company A*	*Expected turnover during first 3 months of process*	*Promotions and transfers that have already been defined*	*Forecast*	*Headcount Company B*	*Expected turnover during first 3 months of process*	*Promotions and transfers that have already been defined*	*Forecast*	
Top Management	6	−1	0	5	4	−3	0	1	6
Sr Mgmt Sales	11	−2	1	10	8	−3	+1	6	16
Mgmt Sales	30	−5	−1/+3	27	22	−4	−1	19	46
Salesforce	422	−60	−3	359	240	−25	0	215	574
Sr Mgmt Support	3	−1	0	2	3	−1	0	2	4
Mgmt Support	15	−2	+2	15	18	−2	0	16	31
Support Staff	90	−10	−2	78	70	−5	0	65	143
Mgmt Technical	3	−1	0	2	4	−2	0	2	4
Technical Staff	35	−3	0	32	30	−3	0	27	59
Total	615	−85	−6/+6	530	399	−48	+1/−1	353	883

Table 6   *Assessing HR over and under staffing areas*

Category	Planned global headcount according to needs	Available headcount	Known or expected* unsuitability between A and B	Over/under staffing
Top Management	6	6	2	2
Sr Mgmt Sales	9	16	2	7
Mgmt Sales	33	46	5	13
Salesforce	530	574	20	44
Sr Mgmt Support	3	4	0	1
Mgmt Support	17	31	2	14
Support Staff	100	143	14	43
Mgmt Technical	3	4	0	1
Technical Staff	40	59	0	19
Total	741	883	45	144

* This refers to staff who have already been identified as non-performers prior to the merger or have acknowledged that they would not have the necessary qualifications for the new position

Table 7   *Impact analysis of a special limited non-termination agreement*

Category	Headcount Company A	Headcount Company B	Total planned redundancies	Maximum acceptable in Company B and in line with plan
Top Management	6	4	2	2
Sr Mgmt Sales	11	8	7	3
Mgmt Sales	30	22	13	8
Salesforce	422	240	44	44
Sr Mgmt Support	3	3	1	1
Mgmt Support	15	18	14	7
Support Staff	90	70	43	25
Mgmt Technical	3	4	1	1
Technical Staff	35	30	19	11
Total	615	399	144	102
Acceptable total				**80**

The fact of identifying non-performers will of course help you to determine appointments and transfers, and identify departments that will need more attention than others. However, it will not allow you to terminate people on the grounds of underperformance. Indeed, most European legislations define collective dismissals as the termination of a given number or percentage of employees *over a definite period of time* (generally three months or more), a period during which attempting to terminate employees on the grounds of underperformance will be considered by most labour courts as the employer's attempt to avoid paying the indemnities attached to collective dismissals.

In many M&As, there are often agreements under which the buyer agrees not to terminate more than a certain percentage of the seller's staff. This percentage is sometimes broken down into specific categories. This practice is only acceptable when the specific categories are not linked to discriminatory factors such as age, gender, race, and so on.

As an example, let us consider a case where it has been agreed that no more than 20 per cent of the staff as a whole, and no more than 35 per cent of staff in any given category may be made redundant on the grounds of the merger. Table 6 will then enable you to prepare a first informal split between the companies and identify some key issues which will need careful examination during the assessment process.

Table 7 shows quite clearly some of the trade-offs that will need to be made, particularly when looking at the sales function. Indeed, simply terminating the salesforce of the acquired company would make little sense. As a result, less than 20 per cent of Company B's staff may be made redundant! This also implies that in this case, perhaps 10 per cent of company A's staff will need to be made redundant as well.

This sort of manpower planning is straightforward and simple. It has the advantage of being easily adaptable to most situations, and can be broken down from the macro corporate view to the micro unit level.

Depending on the company's strategy, it can be fine-tuned to analyse competencies needed versus competencies available in each position (or group). As a result, it can be extended to non-managerial staff and include – either in a redundancy or a mobility programme – all levels of the hierarchy.

In the example below, based on a points assessment, you get a slightly different distribution than the previous example. For help without an assessment system see Table 8. With the help of an assessment system see Table 9.

In Table 9 notice how the assessments change the amount of terminations to consider in the different categories. This results from integrating the figures for promotions in the process and is calculated as follows: (for Mgmt Sales) 46 (staff) -2 (promotions) $+3$ (promotions from below) -33 (available positions) $= 14$ likely redundancies.

Table 8   *Termination analysis without using an assessment system*

Category	Planned global headcount according to needs	Available headcount	Known or expected unsuitability between A and B	Over/under staffing
Sr Mgmt Sales	9	10	2	1
Mgmt Sales	33	46	5	13
Salesforce	530	574	20	44
Total	572	630	27	58

Table 9 *Termination analysis using an assessment system*

Category	Planned global headcount according to needs	Available headcount	Known or expected unsuitability between A and B	Points to qualify	Staff qualifying (unsuitable staff already included)	Staff qualifying for upper level	Terminations or transfers
Sr Mgmt Sales	9	10	2	170	3	0	3
Mgmt Sales	33	46	5	145	37	2	14
Salesforce	530	574	20	120	537	3	41
Total	572	630	27		577	5	58

Another approach, which can also be combined with the points system, uses *required work standards* or widgets per hour and management ratios. This is done when clear ratios exist between productivity and manpower requirement, and between each category of professional staff. The same company has made a forecast of its sales expectations after the merger and determined the salesforce needed to reach those objectives. On this basis, the business ratios governing the quantity of support and management staff throw light on different areas of concern.

The added advantage of this approach is that it can easily be broken down country-by-country to take into account the economic conditions of each region, without changing the company's guidelines on headcount ratios. This allows a very rational approach to the planned reorganization.

Chapter 3
Assessment programmes

Another sensitive part of successful HR integration involves assigning roles and responsibilities within the new organizational structure.

Although it often happens that the acquiring company's structure is kept or imposed as the reference, this is not an immovable standard and an acquisition is an ideal opportunity in a corporation's life to question its operational models.

In the early chapters of this book, I mentioned the importance of understanding the rationale behind the deal. It is at this stage in the process, when a good understanding is extremely useful in helping you define whether your organization is applying an acquisition strategy to achieve international growth, or already has strong international presence, that you will quickly need to either define new, or merge existing international sales and reporting structures.

It may very well be that the structure of the two organizations are similar and that the key challenge will be choosing the right leaders for the right roles. However, you may also be faced with one company with a *market strategy* versus the other with a *business ownership* strategy.

In the *Market Strategy* organization, sales are organized and divided around territories; an Area Manager is responsible for the success of all sales in at least one (if not more) specific market(s).

In the *Business Ownership Strategy*, sales are organized by product group: Product Managers are responsible for specific products across a global market.

At first sight, you may think that merging the first two strategies into one would be the quickest and most efficient approach. I believe that in the majority of cases, introducing a third dimension in a matrix organization (i.e. differentiated territorial, sales and product responsibilities), particularly at this moment in time, is like trying to solve the Rubik's Cube puzzle on a ticking time-bomb; it is generally safer to choose either one or the other route than attempting to combine different systems.

In previous chapters we examined the different stages of organizing merger and acquisition through understanding sales and back-office processes, product mix and customer care, and the reporting systems attached to each. Stemming from this process, we established preliminary job descriptions, objectives and levels of responsibilities of the different positions in the organizations.

The following guidelines review the different steps in the process of assessing employees to identify who should stay and who should go.

The scope and timing of the assessment

The scope and timing of the assessment includes two key processes.

Defining:

1. The population to be assessed (who and how many), and
2. The geographical coverage (will the assessment be conducted in all countries or only at company headquarters, national or international entities).

Defining the population to be assessed

The assessment process tends to divide neatly into two or three stages, each involving a different group of people, different processes and timescales.

The first part of the process is designed to help identify key players in the integration process and happens within the first few weeks following the announcement of the deal. It is limited to a small group of people, needs to be carried out swiftly, and generally has, at the time, little – if any – impact on job security of the individuals assessed.

The second is designed to identify division and line managers, and carried out immediately after the preliminary drafting of the organization chart. These assessments are followed shortly by announcements of new management appointments, and redundancies, with all the emotional turmoil such news invariably creates. Quality of communication is crucial. See Box 2.

Box 2: When equality kills loyalty

In one company, each time an acquisition took place, all employees from both the acquiring and acquired entity had to go through an assessment and suitability programme.

This was meant to indicate that the buyer treated all staff equally in the selection process following the acquisition.

After going through three mergers and acquisitions in two years, accompanied by a raft of terminations and redundancies, surviving personnel of the acquiring company considered that if they had to put their jobs on the line and undergo an assessment every single time their employer bought a new firm, then the concept of loyalty (which is normally expected from both employer and employee) was just not a corporate value here.

> As a result, managers and employees of the acquiring company concluded there was nothing to gain in remaining with a corporation who cared so little about loyalty.
>
> Regardless of the outcome of the assessments, they started looking for other jobs outside the company.

Finally, the third part of the process applies to the whole organization and normally manifests the following positive and negative features.

Positive features:

- There is a standard process throughout the organization
- The assessment offers objective tools for managers to work with when selecting their teams
- The process is an efficient break to clan forming, favouritism and bullying.

Negative features:

- The process is long and expensive and runs the risk that some decisions may need to be made before the assessments are fully completed (which will severely undermine the credibility of the process and of those who initiated it)
- International assessments can be cumbersome, as you try to balance different languages and different legal requirements
- There is only a limited analysis of group synergy factors. As a result, putting together top scoring employees does not guarantee top group performance.

> Defining the geographical coverage.

Conducting a pan-European or international assessment requires attention to a number of points, often overlooked when launching the project, which can become major hurdles. See Box 3 for a pre-assessment checklist to help you identify these:

Box 3: Pre-assessment checklist

- What Human Resources (internal or external) will you need – both in terms of number of people, language skills and competence level – to conduct an international assessment within the set deadlines?
- Is the assessment available in the language of all countries where it will be conducted?
- What are the local legal constraints in conducting the assessments, for example:

- What are the requirements for feedback?
- What is the legal validity of the assessment data, in case of termination?
- How should questions be phrased to ensure their acceptability (in the case of any privacy issues)?
- and so on.
• Have the individuals who will be assessed been identified?
• Has their mother tongue or perfect fluency in a second language been specified? And does it match with the resources available?
• Have these individuals been personally and appropriately informed about:
  - the process
  - the objective and outcome of the assessment
  - the feedback they will receive
  - the timing of the assessment
  - the contact person should they have questions
• Have the managers of the assessed been informed of the process and on how they will be involved in providing feedback?

Key leadership competencies

Whether you decide to conduct assessments yourself, or use an external consultant, you will still need to define the assessment criteria.

The list of leadership skills required in management positions is generally very similar from one position to another. What varies widely is the relative importance given to each quality. For example, the weighting given to strategic thinking will probably vary considerably between a sales manager – who must have the ability to conceive a product campaign for example – and a senior controller who will not require the same skills to check out the validity of financial reports; presentation skills will have greater importance for the marketing director than for the IT director; and superior problem solving qualities will be required for the legal adviser, whereas they may be less important for the business development manager.

Before carrying out a management evaluation, you need to define what core skills are required for the different positions or management groups, and how to analyse the scores attached to the different weightings.

One common approach is to set 10 to 15 key requirements grouped into three main categories for each specific population to be assessed. This population may be defined either in terms of management or of professional expertise. You may want to assess a management team i.e. in terms of leadership, integrity, communication, etc., or specialized professional groups, i.e. sales managers, finance managers, and so on. Each requirement is then rated.

The following example uses the position of an international sales director. Table 10 illustrates the basic assessment of the position. Table 11 highlights the

Table 10   *Basic assessment of the position (manages 12 area sales directors)*

Key criteria	Grade range requirement				W
Business development					
Business acumen	1–10				
Strategic thinking	1–10				
P&L Management	1–10				
Presentation skills	1–10				
Technical skills	1–10				
Management					
Leadership ability	1–5				
Decision making	1–5				
Writing/Communication skills	1–5				
Problem solving	1–5				
Integrity	1–5				
Personal					
Intellectual aptitude	1–3				
Creativity	1–3				
Willingness to travel	1–3				
Willingness to relocate	1–3				
Language skills	1–3				
Score					

	Below average	Average	Above average
Business Development	1–6	7–8	9–10
Management	1–3	4	5
Personal	1	2	3

scoring of an internal candidate. Table 12 shows the results of five candidates from whom the top three have similar scores, and provides two separate techniques for identifying the best candidate.

Depending on how sophisticated you want your analysis to be, you may choose to include weighting factors for each criteria, or exclusion rules (i.e. anybody with more than two criteria below average in the same group is automatically disqualified), or combine the data with other analyses.

Once you have defined the competencies, you will then need to decide who conducts the assessment, and how this will be managed. One of the advantages of using external consultants is that they will provide you with a group of professionals trained in a consistent, structured and objective approach. However, your own HR department may also conduct such an assessment, particularly as a coach to managers grading their subordinates.

Assessing the results

There are a number of different techniques and approaches that can be used for assessment. The most common involve a combination of face-to-face interviews and personality tests.

In the assessment data below and in Table 11, rating points reflect the scored evidence of the assessed criteria. Whatever system you are using, you will need to

Table 11 *Revised assessment of the position*

Position	International Sales Director					
Candidate	Andrew Blade					
Key responsibilities	Defines international sales strategy; ensures growth of market share, monitors success of marketing campaigns, coordinates key accounts management Manages 12 area sales directors					
Key criteria	*Grade range requirement*	*Andrew*				*W*
Business development						
Business acumen	1–10	7				
Strategic thinking	1–10	7				
P&L Management	1–10	8				
Presentation skills	1–10	7				
Technical skills	1–10	8				
Score		37				
Management						
Leadership ability	1–5	3				
Decision making	1–5	3				
Writing/Communication skills	1–5	3				
Problem solving	1–5	3				
Integrity	1–5	4				
Score		16				
Personal						
Intellectual aptitude	1–3	3				
Creativity	1–3	3				
Willingness to travel	1–3	2				
Willingness to relocate	1–3	1				
Language skills	1–3	1				
Score		10				
Total Score		63				

	Below average	Average	Above average
Business Development	1–6	7–8	9–10
Management	1–3	4	5
Personal	1	2	3

break down each criteria into measurable evidence which is then reported on a scoring sheet.

When discrepancies between scorings are significant, the assessment process is easy. It becomes trickier when the scores are tied. See Table 12.

Doing a straight count, you would easily rule out the first two candidates, Andrew and Barbara. However with only 1 point separating Doris from Chris and Eric, each having an equal score, you might want to give it some more thought.

Table 12 *Final assessment of the position*

Position	International Sales Director						
Candidates	Andrew; Barbara; Chris; Doris; Eric						
Key responsibilities	Defines international sales strategy; ensures growth of market share, monitors success of marketing campaigns, coordinates key accounts management Manages 12 area sales directors						
Key Criteria	*Grade range requirement*	*Andrew*	*Barbara*	*Chris*	*Doris*	*Eric*	*W*
Business dev.							
Business acumen	1–10	7	8	9	10	8	
Strategic thinking	1–10	7	8	8	9	7	
P&L Management	1–10	8	7	9	9	9	
Presentation skills	1–10	7	8	8	9	9	
Technical skills	1–10	8	8	8	9	8	
Score		37	39	42	46	41	
Management							
Leadership ability	1–5	3	4	4	4	5	
Decision making	1–5	3	3	4	5	5	
Writing/Com. Skills	1–5	3	3	4	3	3	
Problem solving	1–5	3	4	4	4	3	
Integrity	1–5	4	3	4	5	5	
Score		16	17	20	21	21	
Personal							
Intellectual aptitude	1–3	3	2	3	3	2	
Creativity	1–3	3	2	2	2	2	
Willingness to travel	1–3	2	3	3	2	3	
Willingness to relocate	1–3	1	2	3	1	3	
Language skills	1–3	1	2	2	1	3	
Score		10	11	13	9	13	
Total Score		63	67	75	76	75	

	Below average	Average	Above average
Business Development	1–6	7–8	9–10
Management	1–3	4	5
Personal	1	2	3

Simply on the basis of the scores, Doris should get the job. Let us check she does not have weaknesses that would disqualify her.

Chris = no weaknesses
Doris = 3 weaknesses (but not all three in the same category)
Eric = 2 weaknesses

Based on this, you may want to give a closer look to the differences between these three candidates. One system you might use is to give a weighting to the score of the different categories by order of importance, and then comparing the results again.

Business development = 3
Management   = 2
Personal   = 1

Resulting in:

Chris $42 \times 3 + 20 \times 2 + 13 \times 1 = 178$
Doris $46 \times 3 + 21 \times 2 + 9 \times 1 = 189$
Eric $41 \times 3 + 21 \times 2 + 13 \times 1 = 178$

This time, Doris comes out more clearly as candidate number 1. But who would be candidate number 2 (if Doris were to decline the job) and how significant are Doris' weaknesses?

There is one system, based on multiple-choice analysis, that has the advantage of combining all of the above in a mathematical approach, which can be easily computerized, may focus on all criteria or a selection of them, and provides objective output. Here's how it works:

We have identified and weighted three criteria:

a) Business development weight = 3
b) Management   weight = 2
c) Personal skills   weight = 1

The sum of the weighting criteria is $3+2+1 = 6$

- If we compare the competence of Doris and Chris we get the following result:

$W^+_{Doris/Chris}$ = $3+2 = 5$ The sum of the weighted criteria for the areas in which Doris outperforms Chris (in this case, business development and management)

$W^-_{Doris/Chris}$ = 1 The sum of the weighted criteria where Doris is not as good as Chris (in the area of personal skills)

$W^=_{Doris/Chris}$ = 0 The sum of the weighted criteria where Doris is as good as Chris

$$\frac{W^+_{Doris/Chris}}{W^-_{Doris/Chris}} = \frac{5}{1} \text{ or 5:1 ratio}$$

$$\frac{W^+_{Doris/Chris} + W^=_{Doris/Chris}}{\Sigma\, W_{Doris/Chris}} = \frac{5}{6} \text{ or 83\% of maximum}$$

In this case, Doris' competence exceeds Chris in both instances.
You get the same results comparing her results to those of Eric.

*   If we compare the competence of Chris and Eric, we get:

$W^+_{Chris/Eric}$ = 3 The sum of the weighted criteria for the areas in which Chris outperforms Eric

$W^-_{Chris/Eric}$ = 2 The sum of weighted criteria where Chris is not as good as Eric (management)

$W^=_{Chris/Eric}$ = 1 The sum of weighting criteria where Chris is as good as Eric (personal skills)

$$\frac{W^+_{Chris/Eric}}{W^-_{Chris/Eric}} = \frac{3}{2} \text{ or 3:2 ratio}$$

$$\frac{W^+_{Chris/Eric} + W^=_{Chris/Eric}}{\Sigma W_{Chris/Eric}} = \frac{4}{6} \text{ or 66.7\% of maximum}$$

Both statistics indicate that Chris is better qualified than Eric, although their final scores are identical.

This technique can be used for each and every criteria, in order to better identify the varying discrepancies in selected fields. A summarized example follows where each field is weighted and then compared. See also Table 13.

Does Doris have a slight or big advantage over Chris?

Business development	Management	Personal skills
Doris > Chris = 3+2+2+1 = 8	D > C = 2+3 = 5	D > C = 0
Doris = Chris = 3	D = C = 3+2 = 5	D = C = 2+2=4
Doris < Chris = 0	D < C = 3	D < C = 3+1+2=6
Ratio = 8:0	Ratio = 5:3	Ratio = 0:6
% D >= C = 8 + 3 / 11 = 100%	% of D>=C = 5+5/13 = 77%	% D>=C=4/10 = 40%

From this example, you are safe to conclude that Doris clearly outweighs Chris except in the personal criteria which may need a closer look, in view of the job requirements.

How does Chris compare to Eric?

Business development
Chris > Eric = 3+2 = 5
Chris = Eric = 3+1 = 4
Chris < Eric = 2
Ratio = 5:2
% C>=E = 9/11 = 82%

Management
C > E = 3+2 = 5
C = E = 0
C < E = 3+2+3 = 8
Ratio = 5:8
% C>=E = 5/13 = 38%

Personal skills
C > E = 2
C = E = 2 + 3 + 1 = 6
C < E = 2
Ratio = 2:2 = 1:1
% C>=E=8/10 = 80%

Table 13   *Final scorecard assessment*

Position	International Sales Director										
Candidate	Andrew Barbara Chris Doris Eric										
Key responsibilities	Defines international sales strategy; ensures growth of market share, monitors success of marketing campaigns, coordinates key accounts management Manages 12 area sales directors										
Key Criteria	*Grade range requirement*	*Andrew score *W*		*Barbara score *W*		*Chris score *W*		*Doris score *W*		*Eric score *W*		*Weight*
Business dev.											
Business acumen	1–10	7	21	8	24	9	27	10	30	8	24	3
Strategic thinking	1–10	7	14	8	16	8	16	9	18	7	14	2
P&L Management	1–10	8	24	7	21	9	27	9	27	9	27	3
Presentation skills	1–10	7	14	8	16	8	16	9	18	9	18	2
Technical skills	1–10	8	8	8	8	8	8	9	9	8	8	1
Score		37	81	39	85	42	94	46	102	41	91	
Management											
Leadership ability	1–5	3	9	4	12	4	12	4	12	5	15	3
Decision making	1–5	3	6	3	6	4	8	5	10	5	10	2
Writing/Com. Skills	1–5	3	9	3	9	4	12	3	9	3	9	3
Problem solving	1–5	3	6	4	8	4	8	4	8	3	6	2
Integrity	1–5	4	12	3	9	4	12	5	15	5	15	3
Score		16	42	17	44	20	52	21	54	21	55	
Personal											
Intellectual aptitude	1–3	3	6	2	4	3	6	3	6	2	4	2
Creativity	1–3	3	6	2	4	2	4	2	4	2	4	2
Willingness to travel	1–3	2	6	3	9	3	9	2	6	3	9	3
Willingness to relocate	1–3	1	1	2	2	3	3	1	1	3	3	1
Language skills	1–3	1	2	2	4	2	4	1	2	3	6	2
Score		10	21	11	23	13	26	9	19	13	26	
Total Score		63	144	67	152	75	172	76	175	75	172	
Total Weighted score		144		152		172		175		172		

	Below average	Average	Above average
Business Development	1–6	7–8	9–10
Management	1–3	4	5
Personal	1	2	3

In this example, you may argue that Chris is not as good in Management as Eric and just as good as him in Personal skills. So how can we be sure about Chris' better fit? Using the same weighting factors again on the ratios, you would get:

for Chris $3*5 + 2*5 + 1*2 = 27$
for Eric $3*2 + 2*8 + 1*2 = 24$

It is therefore safe to conclude that Chris closer meets the requirements than Eric.

Feedback and communication on decisions

Once the global exercise is over, you need to provide feedback. As a rule, feedback should be given in two stages. The first stage is designed to communicate to the individuals the results of their scoring and of any personality tests, and also to question:

a) Whether the candidate would consider other positions within the company, and

b) What would their key areas of priority be, if they were appointed to the position they are being considered for?

The second stage, once the decision is taken, is to communicate first to the parties involved, and after that, to the rest of the company, explaining the new reporting lines and the implications the appointment will have on the organization's structure.

Chapter 4

Redundancy strategy and guidelines

Once your manpower plan and assessments are completed, and the employees to be made redundant (or faced with alternative employment opportunities) have been identified, you still need to:

1. Check you are in line with local labour law.
2. Prepare a communication plan.
3. Assign responsibilities.
4. Establish the severance package guidelines.
5. Establish the redundancy guidelines, and
6. Implement a help desk.

Awareness of local labour laws and regulations

This issue might seem obvious; however, in light of recurrent media stories such as the experience of Marks & Spencer in France in the autumn of 2001, you need to remember how different redundancy law can be in the various European countries, and how failure to comply with such law will generally lead to disaster.

This does not mean that every single procedure must always be followed to the letter in every single case; indeed in some situations, general agreements can work. However, before choosing an alternative path, or simply taking for granted that an approach that proved successful in country A will prove equally appropriate in country B, make sure – preferably with the assistance of local legal advice – that the alternative plan you have may not have unforeseen consequences.

To illustrate some of the differences, Table 14 reviews redundancy and termination procedures in Belgium, England, France, Germany and Italy, and Switzerland (as a non-European Union country). Please note that this table is provided here as an overview and should in no way be considered as a complete legal guide to redundancy law in the countries listed.

Table 14 *Analysis of requirements for redundancies in various European countries*

Redundancy situation	Selection	Consultation and procedure	Notice	Payment/indemnity	Additional formalities	Potential liability
Belgium Collective redundancy and plant closure, on economic or technical grounds*	Selection criteria must not discriminate on grounds of race, gender, trade union activity, etc. Assessment based on objective evaluation of skills should be acceptable	Works Council or trade union or, in the absence of both, with employees or informal representatives Aim to consider ways to avoid or reduce collective redundancies. Decision to make collective redundancies must not appear to be set in stone Employer to confirm in writing to the Director of the Regional Employment Office that they intend to proceed with collective redundancies Employer to provide written report notifying intention to proceed with collective redundancy (copy to Director of Regional Employment Office) Report to include: • Reasons • Selection criteria • Number and categories of employees • Calculations of non-statutory redundancy payments • Period of consultation The employer has the obligation to consider proposals of employees or their representatives	30 day cooling off period from the date of the employer's written confirmation to the Director of the Regional Employment Office that they intend to make collective redundancies. Director of the Regional Employment Office may extend cooling off period by up to 30 days	Special payment for collective redundancy 50% of the difference between unemployment benefit/ net salary in new employment and the gross salary (capped at BEF100,000 per month) paid by the employer less social security and tax contributions Severance pay in lieu of notice - lump sum payment for full or remaining duration of notice period to include all contractual benefits and 13th month bonus	Employer must give the employee the following documents on termination of employment: Certificate of Employment; Unemployment Certificate; Holiday Certificate which indicates holiday pay received by employee; Statement of salary due; Individual account for the current year; Salary slip 281 attached to employee's tax return; Proof of payment of the contributions for health insurance	Sanctions for failure to consult on the basis that the employer has failed to observe the consultation and notification procedure

	Redundancy situation	Selection	Consultation and procedure	Notice	Payment/indemnity	Additional formalities	Potential liability
England	A requirement for fewer employees for economic reasons will be a reason for redundancy as opposed to dismissal Establish that: • Circumstances constitute redundancy You have: • Acted reasonably in treating redundancy as reasons for dismissal • Acted fairly in all respects • Complied with consultation and notification procedures	The assessment: core competencies are likely to amount to objective criteria if they can be measured objectively	Must consult on an individual basis to include: • Need for redundancies • Proposed timing • Alternative employment • Feedback Collective consultation with trade unions, representatives or individuals must begin 30 days prior to dismissal if 20–99 employees are affected by redundancy 90 days prior to dismissal if 100 or more employees are affected by redundancy Consult with a view to: • Avoiding dismissals • Reducing numbers of employees made redundant • Mitigating the consequences of dismissal Identify the pool of potentially redundant employees Select on objective criteria Consult Consider alternative employment Collective Redundancy – Election of Employee Representatives	Contractual notice or if contractual notice is less than statutory notice, statutory notice will apply Statutory notice of 1 week for each year of complete service up to a maximum of 12 weeks Can pay, in lieu of notice, for pay and contractual benefits due under the contract of employment	Statutory redundancy payment if continuously employed for 2 years • ½ week's pay for each year of continuous service between ages 18 and 21 • 1 week's pay (£240 max) for each year of continuous employment between ages 22 and 40 • 1½ week's pay (weeks pay = £240 max) for each year of continuous employment over age of 41 • Subject to a maximum of 20 years service	Notify dismissal in a collective redundancy situation Must give written particulars of the calculations of redundancy payment	All payments due under the contract of employment in respect of the notice period. If they are unpaid, employees with one year's continuous employment may claim unfair dismissal Basic Award (calculated in the same way as a statutory redundancy payment) up to maximum of £7200 Compensatory award up to maximum of £51,700. Payment of Protective award for failure to consult or allow election of ER's – not subject to any qualifying criteria of employment

* employee representatives

Table 14   *Analysis of requirements for redundancies in various European countries (continued)*

	Redundancy situation	Selection	Consultation and procedure	Notice	Payment/indemnity	Additional formalities	Potential liability
France	Suppression or transformation of the post or substantial modification of the employment contract linked to economic difficulties or technological changes Prior to making an employee redundant the employer must look for alternative employment within the company or group. If this obligation is not met the dismissal will be deemed to be without cause	French Labour Code sets out core selection criteria: • Family situation (number of children, marital status) • Seniority in the company (length of service) • Particular social situation of some employees (age, disability) • Professional qualifications • Additional criteria may be added by collective agreement (if any exist)	**<10 employees** Employer must consult employee representatives prior to decision to dismiss Provide employees or their representatives with all useful information pertaining to the redundancy situation to include: • Reasons • Number of employees employed • Number of proposed redundancies • Selection criteria • Timescale **>10 employees to be made redundant** Employer must establish Social Plan which must provide for avoidance or limitation of the number of employees to be made redundant Social Plan must offer some but not necessarily all of the following: • Details of outplacement • Assistance to the employee in creating a company • Increased payments **Consultation** **<10 employees** Having informed the ER must arrange individual preliminary meetings with employees **>10 employees** Must inform ERs prior to decision to make redundancies Provide all useful information Communicate provisions of the Social Plan Consultation with ERs which must cover: 1) Measures which will have an impact on the workforce; and 2) Consultation on the redundancy There must be 14 days or more between 1) and 2) **Timing** If less than 10 employees are to be be made redundant the ER must be informed and invited to a meeting with management no less than 3 days before the decision is made final and communicated to the affected employee	Notification of redundancy must not be made prior to the expiry of 7 days from the meeting between the employer and individual meetings Such notification must be in writing and must set out the economic reasons for termination Must notify the DDTE (labour administration) within 8 days of notification of termination of employment	Redundancy payment = 1/10 of monthly gross salary per year of seniority after 2 years of continuous service Plus notice of: • 1–2 months - non-executive employees • 3 months for executives	Where 10 or more employees to be made redundant – the employer must provide the same information to the Labour Administration as it does to the ERs	If the dismissals are held to be wrongful by a court, the court may grant payments ranging from 6 months to 2 years gross salary Failure to consult can render a redundancy unlawful, allowing an employee to claim for wrongful dismissal There are also penalties for failing to consult ER's and failing to notify the Labour Administration

	Redundancy situation	Selection	Consultation and procedure	Notice	Payment/indemnity	Additional formalities	Potential liability
Germany	Plant closure, drop in orders, rationalization may be compelling business reasons which satisfy the requirement for social justification of termination of employment. Termination must be the last resort once the employer has exhausted all other reasonable alternatives – transfer, re-assignment, training for other jobs in the company	Social selection criteria should be used such as age, years of service, number of dependants	The employer must notify the Works Council (if any) of the planned termination In the event of mass layoff of employees at an establishment of 240 or more employees – where 20% or 37 or more employees to be dismissed – detailed rules of consultation with Works Council (if any) apply In addition must negotiate on a 'balance of interest agreement' (governs how dismissals will be carried out) and social plan (governs severance payments based on negotiated formula) Where 10% or more than 25 employees in an establishment of 60–499 are affected, you must notify the Employment Authority within 30 days	Contractual notice or statutory notice, which ever is the greater Statutory notice ranges from 4 weeks in first 2 years of service to a maximum of 7 months after 20 years of service There is no entitlement to payment in lieu of notice unless provided for in the employment contract	Statutory notice ranges from 4 weeks in first 2 years of service to a maximum of 7 months after 20 years of service		
Italy	Reorganization or restructuring whether required by financial difficulties, reduction or transformation of employees' work (for economic or organizational reasons)	Must relate to technical, manufacturing and organizational needs in conjunction with: • Number of family dependants • Salary • Seniority • Technical, manufacturing and organizational needs of the business	Employer must notify trade unions, employee representatives and Labour Office (UPLMO) Notification must include: • Technical and/or organizational reasons • Number and qualifications of employees to be made redundant • Timing of dismissals 7 days from receipt of notification, company employer must meet with unions Agreement must be reached within 45 days. UPLMO can extend time of review consultation Dismissals made within 120 days from start of redundancy procedure will be deemed to be for redundancy	Depends on Seniority and Qualification of employee Employer can only give notice once they have exhausted procedure	Redundancy payment, calculated by reference to seniority of employee Pay share of 13th and 14th month salaries and accrued holiday entitlement May have to pay National Security Office Employer Contribution (9 x monthly unemployment indemnity, ITL1,471,238)	Documents on termination • letter of termination • Employee's Book 'indemnita di mobilita'	Dismissal may be invalid if you fail to consult with unions Failure to adopt lawful procedure may result in the dismissal being null and void, giving rise to re-instatement of the employee

Table 14 *Analysis of requirements for redundancies in various European countries (continued)*

	Redundancy situation	Selection	Consultation and procedure	Notice	Payment/indemnity	Additional formalities	Potential liability
Switzerland	Collective redundancy is defined by: • a minimum of 10 redundancies in a company which employs 20 to 99 employees • 10% of the workforce in a company with 100 to 300 employees • 30 redundancies in a company employing more than 300 people		When more than 10 employees are made redundant there is an obligation to notify the cantonal authorities The employer must provide employees with: • The reasons for redundancies • The total number of employees in the company • The number of anticipated redundancies • The time frame for programme • A copy of a notice containing the above should be sent to the Cantonal Labour Office • Timeframe (a reasonable procedure would be a few months)	There is no specific redundancy payment Must pay contractual notice and holiday pay			Maximum of 6 months salary if the termination is deemed to be abusive Failure to consult may result in the dismissal being deemed to be abusive with a maximum indemnity of an additional 2 months salary

* Any dismissal on economic or technical grounds over a period of 60 days which affects (a) more than 10 employees in an undertaking which employed > 20 < 100 employees during previous calendar year; or (b) at least 10% of employees in companies where the average number of employees during calendar year prior to dismissal was > 100 but < 300. Plant closure is deemed if permanent cessation of activity of an undertaking or one of its divisions and the number of employees of the undertaking or division decreases below 25% of average number of employees during preceding calendar year.

Preparation for the redundancy announcement

In Chapter 3 of Part I on Communication, we went through the importance of preparing a communication agenda, defining the right audience, and the 'communication code of conduct'. Whether you are making a general announcement – such as communicating the deal – or a specific communication, the same rules apply.

When dealing with redundancies, however, and particularly if faced with the need to communicate across multiple sites, you will need to pay special attention to:

- **Timing**: Generally, it is preferable to communicate the redundancy to all employees concurrently. If this cannot be done in a single location or through teleconferencing, you will need to provide a strict timetable to the managers responsible for communicating the plan in the different location(s)

- **Language**: Language refers not only to the style or wording of contents, but to the importance of having the same message given in the local language and in such a way that no statements may be found inappropriate with regard to local labour law on collective redundancies

- **Appendices**: Before communicating the plan, you should have established all relevant guidelines and appendices, which will be needed by the managers responsible for communicating and executing it locally. This will include items such as:
  - The speech or briefing
  - The managers' level when discussing severance packages
  - Legal requirements
  - Any procedures to follow (particularly with reference to unions, the press, and reporting to HQ)
  - The redundancy process and guidelines
  - The terms of any terminations.

Assigning responsibilities

Terminating employees is a process in its own right, and as with the M&A process requires both a plan and designated managers to execute it.

What is key, is not who needs to announce or perform the redundancies, but who is responsible in each location for ensuring that the process is done properly, and that this person knows precisely what their responsibilities are.

It is important to remember that entrusting a manager with the responsibility of the *process* is not the same as entrusting them with the terminations themselves. As a matter of example, a common approach is to have the local HR manager responsible for briefing and guiding the other managers on how to proceed, and ensuring that the legal requirements and general severance procedures are respected. However, breaking the news and engaging in the termination discussions remain the responsibility of the line managers.

Establishing guidelines for the severance package

Depending on the size of your organization, agreements with unions and the general climate prevailing at the time of termination, you may need to prepare a global set of redundancy terms for each country – most of the time with the approval of the unions – or agree on a termination package for each employee.

In large organizations, the latter alternative is rarely an option, as unions will normally already have assumed a role in the global integration process and will act as representatives for all staff. For smaller companies, however, you may be better off agreeing terms on a one-to-one basis with the designated members of staff. This requires immediate action, and *bullet proof* severance agreements drawn up by local lawyers specializing in labour law, and a well-rehearsed sequence of events.

The guidelines for the severance package should cover the following questions:

- How much above the legal standard termination period is the company prepared to pay?

- How will lost stock options or other financial benefits be compensated for (particularly when this is not a legally prescribed requirement)?

- Can items such as mobile phones, laptops, use of the company car for a set period of time, be 'thrown in' as extra tokens if the negotiation becomes difficult?

- Since terminations are linked to a notice period, how quickly can a terminated employee be relieved of their responsibilities? Offering the employee opportunity to leave work immediately following the agreement of the termination package is a powerful negotiating tool. When handled correctly, employees often prove very willing to help out, if needed, on an *ad hoc* basis – thus reducing the risk of corporate loss of knowledge.

It should also include a list of approved legal advisers, which the MD or HR manager may contact in case of need, along with the redundancy procedure to be followed.

Redundancy guidelines

Therese Eben, quoted in Kenneth Labich 'How to fire people and still sleep at night' (*Fortune Magazine*)[1] gives 10 real-life examples of what not to do when terminating people.

1 Fortune Magazine, June 10, 1996, pp. 65ff.

1. **Don't forget you are a member of the family of man** (A manager asked an employee to fire his own father).
2. **Don't use your employees as pawns in a corporate chess game** (Another manager threatened firing to get results).
3. **Don't fire** '*en masse*' (One company held an assembly to announce firings).
4. **Don't rely on electronic messengers** (Another company cancelled an employee's charge card before they told him he was fired).
5. **Don't use the mailman as your messenger** (Some companies still send pink slips or termination letters without warning).
6. **Don't use the airwaves** (A top glamour magazine told the media it was firing an editor before it told her).
7. **Don't ignore the calendar** (One company fired a man on Take Our Daughter to Work Day – in front of his daughter!).
8. **Don't get personal** (A manager who told an employee he was being laid off for being 'emotionally unstable' witnessed his suicide at the office the next day).
9. **Don't be cruel** (A manager fired an employee while passing him in the hall).
10. **Don't be a hypocrite** (A division head in a *Fortune 500* company encouraged employees to undergo special training and then fired them six months later).

Although it may be difficult to find excuses to justify such attitudes, one of the main reasons for them is ignorance of how to proceed, which will generate a high level of stress and emotion.

Redundancy guidelines, that act both as background information and as the basis for the process, help managers prepare for and conduct the termination process properly and allow you to do so decently. Such guidelines generally include:

- Key issues to keep in mind
- How to prepare, and
- How to proceed.

Box 4 and Box 5 offer sample guidelines you may adapt to your own specific needs.

Box 4: Termination guidelines

Key issues to keep in mind

- The employee should be treated fairly and with respect
- The company needs to fulfil its legal and ethical responsibilities
- The employee should understand the essential information about their status
- The disruption to other employees and to the well running of the organization should be kept to a minimum.

Preparing for termination

General preparation

The definition of 'collective termination' is specific to local laws and regulations, as is the term 'economic reason'. Before embarking on the full-scale briefing of your staff, and the subsequent terminations, please check if the number of people to be laid off, or the grounds for termination, requires a specific process governed by your national labour laws.

In any event:

- Establish in writing the step-by-step procedure to be followed and gather all the documentation you need (and send a copy of the action plan to (*name of the contact person*) in the HR department)
- Follow scrupulously all legal requirements of the termination process
- If you have any doubt, refer to the local legal adviser or to the corporate lawyer (name of the contact person) who can advise you, *before* acting
- If you are required to address the issue with unions, please inform headquarters first and take the necessary steps to be adequately represented and/or prepared for such meetings
- In these cases, collective agreements need approval from headquarters before they are implemented.

Planning when and where to communicate the information

- Make sure all employees are present
- Hold the meeting at a time when you can expect minimal disruption from incoming calls or visits
- Although the meeting should remain as informal and casual as possible, it is inappropriate to organize a drink or other social event, immediately following the announcement
- Obtain legal opinion if you are uncertain of ANY actions.

Planning what to say

- The entire staff must be informed verbally of the reorganisation process, any cost-cutting measures, and their consequences on employment. The communication should be factual, short and concise and not go into personal or emotional considerations
- Make sure that you can answer any likely questions which may arise from that announcement, but remember not to address personal issues in public. It is best to take those 'off-line'
- Set the right tone – be warm, receptive and interested in what employees have to say

- Listen. Don't insert personal comments; provide opinions or defend/condemn the company and its actions. Your role is to communicate information and remain objective
- You may want to have tissue and a glass of water to hand.

Box 5: The termination process

- The termination process should commence as quickly as possible following the announcement and preferably within the next 24 hours
- Whenever possible, the MD should call and conduct the termination meeting
- Prepare for the interview (know the details of the relevant contract and employment conditions and read at least the CV and performance reviews of the employee you are about to terminate)
- Inform the employee that the termination is final and the date from which the termination will be effective
- Let the employee know what benefits (unemployment, insurance, severance pay) are available. State laws typically govern how and when final pay and holiday allowances are handled
- Give the employee a written termination notice, which they need to acknowledge receipt of, without necessarily agreeing to the terms, by signing the notice
- Consider offering assistance to the employee to find another job. You might offer company assistance in preparing and mailing/posting resumés, giving them help with job search coaching tips, outplacement services and so on.

Be prepared to answer questions such as:

- When is my last day?
- When should I leave?
- Will I receive severance pay and how much will it be?
- Will I receive bonuses for which I am eligible?
- When will I receive my last paycheque?
- Will I be paid for any unused holiday allowance?
- Am I eligible for unemployment benefit?
- Who will provide employment references?
- How will my termination be communicated to clients?
- Will my medical and insurance benefits continue?
- When must I return company property such as cellular phone, car, keys, laptop, etc.?
- Can I continue to use my office or work area to look for a job?
- Can I say good-bye to everyone before I go?
- When can I go back to my work area to collect my personal things?

Employee reactions

Employee reactions to being terminated can run the full range of human emotion. Here are a few tips for how to handle strong emotions.

- Never argue with an employee to justify a termination decision. Be courteous, confident and firm
- If an employee becomes emotional, you should allow them ample time to recover. Be prepared to have a glass of water and tissues handy
- If an employee becomes angry, you should state – in a normal tone of voice – that the meeting will not continue until he or she calms down. You should never respond in kind
- If an employee makes threat of a lawsuit you should either not respond or make a neutral comment by way of acknowledgement

---

Implementing a helpdesk or hotline

In larger organizations, the flow of questions and inquiries resulting from layoffs will often swamp the Human Resources Department (or local Managing Director's desk) preventing them from providing fast, complete and efficient feedback.

Different strategies exist to address this issue, the most obvious of which are to provide:

- A hotline. In the majority of cases, merging corporations will use an outsourcing company to provide a hotline service during a set period of time. This enables the company to offer a real-time, around the clock, service to its employees without mobilizing internal resources needed elsewhere.
- An intranet FAQ forum, where employees are invited to ask questions which will be answered both via e-mail, for personal issues, and summarized in a general format on a Q&A page.

The added advantage of a hotline is that outsourcing companies generally provide a multilanguage service, which an intranet service will have more difficulties in providing with limited resources.

Using facilitators, career counselling and outplacement services

Some managers feel it is their responsibility to handle a termination process from A to Z. Others feel uncomfortable about the process, particularly when they have had lasting relationships with the employees they have to terminate. These managers will often welcome the assistance of facilitators.

Although you may feel that good managers should be able to handle terminations effectively, some of your best executives may well benefit from support in executing this difficult task. In the same way that you would be prepared to provide them with support in managing for growth you should be prepared to make support available to them during downsizing.

Ensuring the process is completed fairly and sympathetically should be a key objective.

Many companies consider career counselling or outplacement as part of the severance package. The relevance of this approach is debatable and depends on the basis on which the service is offered. It also requires some form of agreed policy to provide answers for the following questions:

- Will outplacement be offered to all employees (including non-management, junior and professional staff)?
- If this is not the case, what are the criteria to be eligible for the outplacement service?
- Can an eligible employee receive, in lieu of the outplacement service, cash compensation equal to, or representing a sizeable fraction of the outplacement fee if they so choose?
- Can an eligible employee choose another form of assistance or career counselling for a comparable amount, such as a specific training programme or personal counselling?
- Does the outplacement service imply that the employee is considered unfit for any other position the company, or one of its subsidiaries, may have to offer in the immediate future? How is this implication communicated?

Remember to consider local practice when debating whether or not to provide external counselling to employees after termination. This is a common and expected practice in Scandinavia – and more specifically in Sweden – whilst it is less evident elsewhere.

Chapter 5

Finalizing transfers and integration

As you reach the end of the merger process, with the announcement of new appointments, terminations, details of product lines and reorganization, the time has come to address the transfer of employment contracts.

It may also be an appropriate time to conduct a satisfaction survey amongst remaining employees to identify potential areas of concern and define effective corrective action.

Transfers, appointments and lines of reporting

As well as affecting terminations, local regulations govern the transfer of working contracts. As a rule, the acquiring company needs to respect all clauses specifically mentioned in the original employment contract – one of the reasons it is so important to proceed with a full review of such clauses in the Due Diligence process – as unilateral changes are illegal.

There are two principal means to transfer employment rights from one company to another:

1. By confirming the transfer of employment by personalized letter (eventually including amendments)
2. By drafting new contracts for all employees integrated in the new organization with the new terms and conditions, making specific reference to accrued rights such as holidays, pension and seniority (this last point being very important as seniority implies specific benefits in a number of countries).

Of course, local labour law will govern such situations, in the absence of such clauses and in any case of conflict.

Bear in mind that in Europe, limiting the transfer of employment to a circular note stipulating that all employees are now part of the new organization can be disputed in court (even if such a letter stipulates that terms and conditions remain unchanged), as any amendment to the employment contract needs the approval of both parties.

Communication remains a key issue at this time, particularly regarding some of the transitional aspects of the transfer of employment rights, and especially if pension, special insurance, holiday and other benefits are affected by the merger. Remember that the European Union has issued clear directives on the transfer of rights in the event of an acquisition, change of ownership or other events leading to any form of employment transfer. A copy of this directive is presented in Appendix 2.

Integrating employees

One company was great at celebrating the departure of employees. Farewell cocktails, good-bye parties, 'time-to-go' celebrations accompanied by humorous speeches, anecdotes and stories were events that employees were looking forward to, at a time when management should have been focusing on the reasons for their staff turnover which was in excess of 30 per cent. Particularly since the majority of those employees leaving had been with the company for only a short period of time.

Partying, kick-off meetings and celebrations are a vital part of identifying oneself with a community. This identification or integration process starts within the first few days of joining a new workplace. As a new employee, if your first celebration is around the departure of some colleagues, the chances are you will spend more time wondering why some people are so happy to leave rather than why so many are happy to stay.

In a merger and acquisition process, ensuring smooth integration of new colleagues is even more critical and there are a few do's and don'ts to bear in mind. See Box 6 and Box 7.

Box 6: Some 'Do's'

Do:

- Make the first day a celebration by having a proper welcome organized, flowers, a candle – or any other small gesture – ready on the newcomer's desk

- Ensure that the new employee's arrival has been fully announced (ideally with a picture attached to the announcement), their ID logged into the networks, and that they have an operational e-mail, a phone (with the extension on the new phone list), and so on

- Make sure a new employee receives short, realistic and productive objectives for their first week

- If possible, organize an event involving the new employee's family as well, giving the employee a chance to give their relatives either a tour of their new working environment

- Make sure their supervisor has the time (or makes the time) to brief them correctly and assign them to relevant tasks immediately

- Assign a 'buddy' – generally a co-worker – responsible for making sure the new employee gets introduced properly to other colleagues, finds their way around the premises, and gets the proper assistance they require during the first few days

- Where applicable, give the employee the opportunity, during such meetings, to introduce themselves, explain why they are pleased to join the new company, and what their goals and objectives are

- Organize short presentations preferably by division heads (including HR) where products, objectives and processes are described. This would also probably be the right time to make sure the employee has read, understood and signed corporate handbooks and book of procedures

- If possible, organize for the CEO or one of the top senior executives to greet the new employee and shake hands. If this is not feasible, a welcome letter a week or two after the employee has started, stating that the CEO is pleased to hear how smoothly the new employee is integrating is also a very motivating and positive signal to give

- Take the time to meet and follow up with the new employee at least twice during their first three months with the new company and to share feedback with their supervisor.

Box 7: Some 'Don'ts'

Don't:

- Leave the receptionist unaware of any newcomer, unprepared to deal with him or her, when they arrive

- Insist the new employee sign off the 100 page procedure and processes manual, corporate handbook, signature and spending authorisation sheets and special clauses while they wait for their supervisor in reception

- Forget to prepare a working area for the new employee and don't let him or her stand for hours in the corridor while you struggle to find the desk and PC you forgot to order

- Leave new employees unannounced (whether on the intranet or the bulletin board) but, equally, don't spend half the day rushing them through the entire organisation introducing them to everybody including co-workers they will probably have nothing or very little to do with

- Have him or her spend their first full afternoon attending presentation after presentation

- Have the employee start at a time when their supervisor is on holiday

- Leave the employee on their own over lunch without making sure their colleagues have included them in their lunching plans

- Overwhelm him or her with work including tasks which have nothing to do with the job he or she was hired for

- Assign him or her to a 'buddy' who has plenty of time to look after them but whom you know has always had serious doubts about the validity of the merger

- Take it for granted that if you don't hear from the new employee during the first three months, everything is OK.

These points represent only a few, of the many things, to bear in mind. However, applying them, ensuring management is committed and sensitive to a new employee's state of mind, and following up regularly on the progress of the integration will certainly avoid most of the employee dissatisfaction or disillusionment which may occur in the first months following a merger. And if you are welcoming a team, these do's and don'ts are even more important, particularly if you want to avoid clans forming.

Finally, you may want to consider conducting a satisfaction survey in order to get a sense of the general feeling prevailing in the organization and to identify areas that require more of your attention. A number of such surveys exist, either on-line or in paper form. Appendix 2 provides an example of a general survey that can be conducted in either form.

As with the assessments, it is important to make sure the survey is conducted in the local national language.

Although, in some countries, there is no legal obligation to provide feedback on surveys I nevertheless strongly recommend it is given. If the results are positive, it is a good morale boosting tool; if they are negative, it gives you a unique opportunity to communicate to staff that you:

- have been made aware of their areas of concern
- take such concerns seriously
- will be taking corrective measures as soon as possible, and
- will provide feedback on progress made.

In conclusion, the success of the final steps of integration will largely depend on the same factors as the global merger:

- Your ability to communicate and provide feedback in a clear and straight-forward manner
- Your commitment and subsequent actions for addressing areas of concern
- The energy of management to make everyone integrated and key players of a new and exciting project.

Conclusion

In theory, there is no difference between theory and practice. But, in practice, there is.

Jan L.A. van de Snepscheut

The most commonly sought objectives of mergers and acquisition, whether involving small or large organizations are:

- Gaining synergy
- Gaining market penetration
- Gaining visibility
- Increasing productivity
- Increasing knowledge
- Increasing shareholder value
- Improving efficiency
- Improving processes
- Reducing costs.

Few if any of these objectives can be achieved without the commitment, dedication and project-ownership of the Human Resources department.

The Human Resources department must establish its own set of objectives for the success of the process, the foremost of which are:

- **Clarity**: by ensuring that the purpose, objectives and mission of the merger are crystal clear to all affected by it
- **Competence**: by establishing professional teams of committed managers, employees and consultants in a defined and robust organizational process
- **Communication**: recognising that you cannot over-communicate and that ignorance and/or misinformation is damaging
- **Ethics**: by remembering at all times that you are dealing with human beings and that fairness, honesty and shared values are the foundation of any respectable organized society

- **Receptiveness**: by understanding that although heightened emotion is a by-product of change and uncertainty, the same emotion can be a source of creativity
- **Speed of action**: by making sure that solutions or at least answers are given quickly to concerns or problems expressed, and bearing in mind that unaddressed problems will not go away with time but become more pressing
- **Thoroughness**: by assessing each process in detail and not assuming what may initially appear to be a minor issue, will only generate minor concerns.

With public opinion against it, nothing can succeed. With public opinion on its side, nothing can fail.

Abraham Lincoln

Appendices

Appendices

Appendix 1

Employee satisfaction survey © James F. Klein

	Fully agree	Agree	Partly agree	Disagree	Fully disagree
Corporate communication					
The company provides me with the general information I need					
I trust the information communicated to me					
I have confidence in the leadership of the company in my country					
I have confidence in the leadership of the company at headquarters					
I know the company well					
I am satisfied with the way the company communicates with me					
I understand the direction and strategy of the new combined organisation					
The company should communicate better internally on					
Its strategy for the future					
Its products and services					
Its overall financial situation					
Its capabilities					
The Human Resources processes					
Career opportunities					
Benefits					
Compensation and bonus programmes					
Technological developments					
Issues and trends affecting our business					
Key customer business issues					
Company success stories					

	Fully agree	Agree	Partly agree	Disagree	Fully disagree
Competitive initiatives					
Marketing programmes					
Involvement with the community					
Today, I rely strongly on information I get through					
The 'grapevine'					
My supervisor					
Management at my location					
The Managing Director					
Internal communiqués					
The internet					
Company e-mails					
My MD/Manager effectively communicates					
The company's strategic priorities					
What is expected of my department					
What is expected of my performance					
How he/she rates my contribution to the company					
Employee satisfaction					
I am optimistic about the future of the company					
I am optimistic about my future success with the company					
I feel more committed to a career with the company this year than last year					
I feel that the company cares about its people					
I feel that working for the company will lead to the kind of future I want					
I feel that people get ahead primarily on the merits of their own work					
I feel men and women are provided with equal career opportunities					
I feel I have a good understanding of the company's policies, processes and values					
I am satisfied with my understanding of the directions and goals of the company					
I have a clear understanding of how the company's strategy differentiates us from the competition					
I am satisfied with my understanding of how my goals are linked to the goals of the company					
I have adequate information on available training and education programmes					
I have adequate information on available career and job opportunities in the company					
The company is an industry leader in important ways					
The company's senior management has a clear vision of the future					

	Fully agree	Agree	Partly agree	Disagree	Fully disagree
The company's senior management has made changes that are positive for the company					
The company's senior management has made changes that are positive for me					
The company's senior management is responding to the important external issues					
I am enthusiastic and personally committed to the changes					
My managers are positive role models I want to follow					
My managers keep me well informed about what's going on in the company					
My managers care about and respond to the issues that are important to me					
The people I work with are highly professional					
I believe there is a spirit of cooperation within the company					
There's a great team spirit in my work environment					
Morale is high amongst my colleagues					
I have a high level of morale					
I receive appropriate recognition for my contribution					
I have the necessary tools/power to influence the quality of my work					
My financial compensation matches my responsibilities					
I feel secure in my job					
I receive frequent marks of recognition and praise for my work					
I think this is a great place to work					
I am extremely satisfied with my job					
I am much more satisfied with my job today than last year					
I want to stay with the company					
When communicating with my manager					
I feel free to say what I think					
He or she listens attentively					
He or she is accessible when needed					
He or she is responsive to my concerns					
He or she lets me know what is expected of me					
He or she keeps me informed of things I need to know					
He or she lets me do my job without interfering					
He or she gives me the authority I need to do my job					
He or she treats me fairly					
He or she asks me for my input to help make decisions					
He or she shares information on company performance and goals					

Appendix 2

Termination agreements

In the following pages you will find a sample termination/compromise agreement for each of the following countries: Belgium, France, Germany, Italy, Switzerland, United Kingdom. These agreements include the standard style, terms and topics for each country. At the end of the sample, you will also find an annexe with additional points for consideration which may need to be integrated in the compromise agreements

In the 'comparative analysis of requirements for redundancies in various European countries' (Chapter 4 of Part III), the procedure for terminating employees on economic grounds varies considerably from one country to another. Consequently, the style and content of compromise agreements will be different too.

The following samples are given as examples. However, and with the exception of Switzerland, where termination of employment is an extremely simple and straightforward process, it is strongly advisable that you work closely with an employment law specialist before engaging in any terminations of employment, whatever the number of employees involved.

Remember that in France all correspondence, contracts and agreements MUST be in French (even if the employee signs a document stating that they are fully fluent in English) to be considered legally binding. For this reason, the attached example is presented in French with an accompanying English translation.

Sample termination agreement: Belgium

SETTLEMENT AGREEMENT

BETWEEN: [name + corporate form of employer], with registered offices located at [address], represented by Mr./Ms. [name + position of person who is legally entitled to execute the settlement agreement on behalf of the employer], hereinafter referred to as 'the Employer',

on the one hand,

AND: Mr./Ms. [name], residing at [address], hereinafter referred to as 'the Employee',

on the other hand;

Preliminary Considerations:

The Employee has been employed by the Employer as '[position]' pursuant to an employment contract of [date];

The Employer has terminated the employment contract of the Employee by registered letter of [date] on the basis of a notice period of [number] months which commences on [date]; [ALTERNATIVELY: The Employer has terminated the employment contract of the Employee on [date] without the observance of a notice period but with the payment of a severance indemnity in lieu of notice];

The parties subsequently met in order to discuss the terms and conditions of the Employee's departure;

The purpose of this Settlement Agreement (the 'Agreement') is to determine these terms and conditions.

IT HAS BEEN AGREED AS FOLLOWS:

I.   **Termination Date**

1.   The Employee's last working day is [date]. The employment contract of [date] between the Employer and the Employee thus ended on [date].

II.   **Indemnity**

2.   At the latest on [date], the Employer will pay:

- the notice period in the gross amount of [amount] €, corresponding to [number] months' salary
- the end-of-employment holiday allowance [IF APPLICABLE: and a <u>pro rata</u> thirteenth month]
- [IF APPLICABLE: an indemnity for collective dismissal for a period of [number] months]

- **[IF APPLICABLE:** the amount of € [   ] corresponding to the contractual Bonus / Commissions for the period starting on [date] and ending on [date].

3. The Employee's social security contributions and the payroll tax will be deducted from all above mentioned amounts. The net amount of this compensation will be paid to the Employee by transfer to his/her bank account No. **[number]** with the **[name of bank]**.

4. Pursuant to Articles 39 and 82 of the Law of 3 July 1978 on Employment Contracts, the Employee agrees and confirms:

   - the amount of the compensation
   - the length of the notice period which this compensation corresponds to
   - the gross annual salary which served as the basis for the calculation of this compensation
   - all other elements of compensation described here above

   and as mentioned in Article 2 of this Agreement.

III. **Return of property**

5. At the latest on **[date]** before 5 PM, the Employee will return to the Employer all of the documents and property which he received from the Employer to perform of his/her duties, including but not limited to **[IF APPLICABLE:** the company car, petrol card, portable PC, mobile phone, mobile phone card, credit card, office keys, laptop ...**]** at the registered offices of the Employer.

6. At the latest on **[date]**, the Employer will transmit to the Employee all social documents, including a C4 form.

IV. **Claims**

7. The parties expressly agree that this Agreement constitutes a settlement within the meaning of Article 2044 <u>et seq.</u> of the Belgian Civil Code.

8. Consequently, on condition of payment by the Employer of the amounts mentioned in Articles 2 of this Agreement, the Employee waives all rights, titles and claims, existing or potential, which he/she could enforce or invoke vis-à-vis the Employer with regard to the conclusion, performance or termination of the employment contract of the Employee, including errors in fact or in law, omissions as to the nature and scope of his/her rights, and 'aggravated injury' (i.e. 'gekwalificeerde benadeling' / 'lésion qualifiée').

9. The above-referenced waiver by the Employee not only concerns the Employer but also all other companies of the [name] group of companies.

10. The Employee expressly acknowledges that he/she signs this Agreement of his/her own free will and without coercion from the Employer.

V. Secrecy and Confidentiality

11. The Employer and the Employee agree that this Agreement will be treated as a confidential agreement and that they will not disclose any information in this respect, either within or outside of the company of the Employer, except to persons who must be informed about the content of this Agreement in order to enforce it.

12. The Employee agrees that he will not make any untrue statement in relation to any Group Company or its offices or staff or make any statement which is intended to or which may have the effect of damaging or lowering the reputation of any Group Company or its officers or staff.

VI. Jurisdiction

13. This Agreement is governed by Belgian law.

14. The Employer and the Employee agree that the Courts of [city] will have exclusive jurisdiction to hear any dispute regarding the validity, the interpretation or the performance of this Agreement.

*

Executed in [place] on [date], in two original copies. Each party acknowledges having received one original copy.

For the Employer,

The Employee
(signature preceded by the
hand-written mention
'read and approved')

_____   _____

[name + position]   [name]

Sample termination agreement: France

ACCORD TRANSACTIONNEL

ENTRE LES SOUSSIGNE/E/S :

La société *[dénomination]*, société *[forme juridique]* au capital de *[montant du capital social]*, dont le siège social est situé à *[adresse]*, inscrite au Registre du Commerce et des Sociétés de *[ville]*, sous le numéro *[1 lettre + 9 chiffres]*, représentée par *[Monsieur ou Madame, prénom, nom]*, *[qualité]*,

D'UNE PART,

ET

[Monsieur ou Madame, prénom, nom], domicilié*[e]* *[adresse]*,

D'AUTRE PART,

PREALABLEMENT A L'OBJET DES PRESENTES, IL A ETE EXPOSE CE QUI SUIT:

Rappel des faits

[Monsieur ou Madame, prénom, nom] a été engagé*[e]* par la société *[dénomination]*, sous contrat de travail à durée indéterminée, à compter du *[date]*, en qualité de *[titre]*, avec le statut *[Ouvrier, Employé, Agent de Maîtrise, Cadre]*, au sens de la Convention Collective Nationale *[intitulé]*.

[décrire les faits]

En conséquence, la société *[dénomination]* a été contrainte d'envisager de procéder au licenciement pour motif économique de *[Monsieur ou Madame, prénom, nom]*, en raison de *[motif du licenciement]*.

COMPROMISE AGREEMENT

BETWEEN THE UNDERSIGNED

The company *[Company Name]*, a *[juridical type of company]* with a Capital of *[amount]*; headquartered at *[address]*; registered in the *"Registre du Commerce et des Sociétés"* (Trade Register) of *[City]* under *[cipher 1 letter + 9 digits]*; and represented by *[Mr or Ms First and Last Name]*; *[function]*

ON ONE HAND,

AND

[Mr or Ms; First and Last Name]; living at *[address]*,

ON THE OTHER HAND

PRIOR TO A MEETING OF THE SIGNATORIES, THE FOLLOWING INFORMATION WAS SET FORTH:

Summary of events

[Mr or Ms; First and Last Name]; was hired on *[date]* by the company *[Company Name]*; with an open-ended contract, in the capacity of *[title]* ; and the status of *[Workman, Employee, Foreman; Manager]* as defined in the National Collective Agreement *[Premises of Collective Agreement]*.

[Describe the facts and events]

Consequently, the company [Company Name] was compelled to consider the termination of employment for economic reasons of *[Mr or Ms; First and Last Name]*; because of *[reason for termination of employment]*

C'est ainsi que la société *[dénomination]* a, par lettre *[remise en propre le [date] ou recommandée avec accusé de réception du [date]]*, convoqué *[Monsieur ou Madame, prénom, nom]* à un entretien préalable en vue d'un éventuel licenciement.

As a result the Company *[Company Name]* summoned *[Mr or Ms; First and Last Name]*; *[by remittance in own hands on [date]; by registered letter with acknowledgment of receipt [date]]* to a preliminary meeting in view of a probable termination of employment.

L'entretien préalable s'est déroulé le *[date]*.

The meeting was held on *[date]*,

Par lettre recommandée avec demande d'avis de réception en date du *[date]*, la société *[dénomination]* a notifié à *[Monsieur ou Madame, prénom, nom]* son licenciement pour motif économique.

On *[date]*, the Company *[Company Name]* notified *[Mr or Ms; First and Last Name]* by registered mail with acknowledgment of receipt of his termination on the grounds of economic reasons.

[le cas échéant, indiquer que le/la salarié(e) à adhéré(e) à la convention de conversion qui lui a été proposée]

[If applicable, indicate that the employee agreed to the terms for termination which were proposed to him/her]

A la suite de la notification de ce licenciement, un désaccord profond est intervenu entre les parties.

The notification of termination subsequently led to a profound disagreement between the parties.

[le cas échéant, indiquer que le/la salarié(e) a saisi ou fait savoir qu'il/elle saisirait le CPH]

[If applicable, indicate that the employee chose or said that he/she would choose to refer the agreement to arbitration]

Argumentation développée par *[Monsieur ou Madame, prénom, nom]*

Arguments put forward by *[Mr or Ms; First and Last Name]*;

[Monsieur ou Madame, prénom, nom] conteste formellement la mesure de licenciement pour motif économique prononcée à son égard.

[Mr or Ms; First and Last Name]; expressly contests the decision to terminate his/her employment for economic reasons.

[décrire les griefs adressés par le/la salarié(e) à la société]

[Describe the basis for the employees refusal to accept the termination decision, that was given to the company]

En conséquence, *[Monsieur ou Madame, prénom, nom]* considère que le licenciement prononcé à son égard par la société *[dénomination]* est dépourvu de cause réelle et sérieuse ce qui lui cause un préjudice très important.

As a result, *[Mr or Ms; First and Last Name]*; considers that the decision to terminate his/her employment rests on no real and serious cause and consequently represents a very serious prejudice against him/her.

[description du préjudice résultant pour le/la salarié(e) de son licenciement]

[description of the prejudice as a consequence of the employee's termination]

Argumentation développée par la société *[dénomination]*

La société *[dénomination]* soutient que le motif invoqué à l'appui du licenciement de *[Monsieur ou Madame, prénom, nom]* présente incontestablement un caractère réel et sérieux.

[description des raisons adressés par la société au/à la salarié(e)]

En conséquence de quoi, à l'issue d'un temps de réflexion et de discussion, les parties, après avoir pris l'exacte mesure de leur désaccord, tant en ce qui concerne le fondement de la rupture de leurs relations contractuelles que de ses conséquences matérielles et morales, et en pleine connaissance de leurs droits respectifs, ont décidé de se faire des concessions réciproques et de mettre fin à leur litige sur la base de l'accord transactionnel et irrévocable dont la teneur suit :

ARTICLE 1

La société *[dénomination]* maintient la décision de licenciement qui a été notifiée à *[Monsieur ou Madame, prénom, nom]* par lettre recommandée avec accusé de réception du *[date]*.

La rupture du contrat de travail de *[Monsieur ou Madame, prénom, nom]* est donc aujourd'hui définitive.

ARTICLE 2

[Monsieur ou Madame, prénom, nom] renonce expressément à demander et à se prévaloir de sa priorité de réembauchage au sein de la société *[dénomination]* et de toute autre société ou entité du groupe *[dénomination]*.

Arguments defended by the Company *[Company Name]*

The Company *[Company Name]* maintains that the grounds for terminating *[Mr or Ms; First and Last Name]*'s employment are, beyond question, of a real and serious nature.

[description of reasons given by the company to the employee]

As a result, and following due time for thought and discussion, both parties, having taken the full measure of their disagreement not only as to the core reasons for the severance of their contractual relations, but also to the subsequent moral and financial consequences thereof, and fully aware and informed of their respective rights thereto, have mutually agreed to make concessions and put an end to their dispute on the basis of the compromise and irrevocable agreement as follows.

ARTICLE 1

The company *[Company Name]* maintains the termination of *[Mr or Ms; First and Last Name]*'s as signified to him/her on *[date]*, by registered mail with acknowledgement of receipt.

The termination of *[Mr or Ms; First and Last Name]*'s is therefore considered today as final.

ARTICLE 2

[Mr or Ms; First and Last Name]'s expressly waives his/her right to request and prevail himself/herself of priority re-employment by the company *[Company Name]* and any other of the Group's *[Group's Name]* subsidiaries or entities.

ARTICLE 3

[A la fin du contrat de travail, soit le [date] ou à la signature des présentes], la société *[dénomination]* remet*[tra]* à *[Monsieur ou Madame, prénom, nom]*, à titre de solde de tout compte, les sommes suivantes *[liste indicative]* :

1. une somme de *[montant]* € bruts au titre de :l'indemnité compensatrice de préavis *[correspondant, le cas échéant, en cas d'acceptation de la convention de conversion, au solde de l'indemnité compensatrice de préavis restant dû au salarié après paiement à l'ASSEDIC, dans la limite de deux mois, de ladite indemnité compensatrice]*,moins les charges sociales afférentes à la somme ci-dessus ;

2. une somme de *[montant]* F bruts au titre de :l'indemnité compensatrice de congés payés correspondant à *[nombre de jours]* de congés payés, moins les charges sociales afférentes à la somme ci-dessus ;

3. une somme de *[montant]* F au titre de :l'indemnité conventionnelle de licenciement prévue par la Convention Collective Nationale *[intitulé]*.

ARTICLE 4

[A la fin du contrat de travail, soit le [date] ou à la signature des présentes], la société *[dénomination]* octroie*[ra]* à *[Monsieur ou Madame, prénom, nom]*, à titre de dommages et intérêts, par remise d'un chèque, une indemnité de *[montant]* F bruts dont il *[a été/sera]* déduit la CSG et la CRDS.

Le règlement susvisé prend notamment en compte :

- l'ancienneté de *[Monsieur ou Madame, prénom, nom]* au sein de la société *[dénomination]* *[indiquer l'ancienneté entre parenthèse]*,

ARTICLE 3

At the end of the employment contract on *[date]* *[alternative: upon signature of this compromise agreement]*, the company *[Company Name]* will pay the following amounts to *[Mr or Ms; First and Last Name]'* as full settlement for all claims.

1. The sum of *[amount]* € gross, in compensation for the notice period *[which corresponds, if such is the case, and if the employee agreed to the professional conversion agreement, to the remainder of the compensating indemnity after payment to the ASSEDIC within the limit of two months.]*, and from which relevant Social Contributions will be withheld.

2. An amount of *[amount]* € gross in compensation for holidays not taken amounting to *[Number of days]* days, and from which relevant Social Contributions will be withheld.

3. An amount of *[amount]*. € as statutory termination indemnity as stated in the National Collective Agreement [Name of Agreement]

ARTICLE 4

At the end of the employment contract on *[date]* *[alternative: upon signature of this compromise agreement]*, the company *[Company Name]* will pay by cheque to order of *[Mr or Ms; First and Last Name]'* in compensation for damages, the sum of *[amount]* € gross from which the CSG and CRDS contributions will have been withheld.

The above mentioned payment takes into account:

- The length of service of *[Mr or Ms; First and Last Name]'* in the Company *[Company Name]* *[indicate the employee's seniority in brackets]*

- son âge *[indiquer l'âge entre parenthèse]*,

- les répercussions professionnelles, morales, psychologiques et familiales de son licenciement,

Cette transaction couvre tous droits, avantages ou indemnités, de quelque nature que ce soit, que *[Monsieur ou Madame, prénom, nom]* pourrait éventuellement faire valoir ou auxquels *[il ou elle]* pourrait prétendre en vertu des dispositions légales, réglementaires ou conventionnelles en vigueur.

ARTICLE 5

[Monsieur ou Madame, prénom, nom] reconnaît que le versement de la somme de *[montant]* € bruts visée à l'article 4 ci-dessus lui est consenti par la société *[dénomination]* pour *[le ou la]* dédommager de tout préjudice subi du fait de la rupture de son contrat de travail.

En conséquence, en contrepartie du versement des sommes visées aux articles 3 et 4 ci-dessus, *[Monsieur ou Madame, prénom, nom]* déclare expressément n'avoir vis-à-vis de la société *[dénomination]* et de toute autre société ou entité du groupe aucune réclamation de quelque nature que ce soit à formuler, renonce à tous ses droits, actions et prétentions du chef de l'exécution et de la rupture du contrat de travail dont s'agit, tant sur le fond que sur la forme.

[Monsieur ou Madame, prénom, nom] déclare être parfaitement averti(e) de sa situation au regard des organismes de Sécurité Sociale, de chômage et de l'Administration Fiscale, et déclare que ces questions ne sauraient en aucun cas remettre en cause les présentes.

[Monsieur ou Madame, prénom, nom] s'engage à se désister, à ses frais, de toute action ou instance qu'*[il ou elle]* a pu engager, devant quelque juridiction que ce

- His/her age *[indicate age in brackets]*

- The repercussions of professional, moral, psychological and private. nature which the termination will have.

This agreement covers all rights, advantages or indemnities, of any sort and whatever they may be, which *[Mr or Ms; First and Last Name]'* could eventually claim or pretend to according to legal, regulatory or statutory dispositions in force.

ARTICLE 5

[Mr or Ms; First and Last Name]' acknowledges that the amount of *[amount]* € gross as mentioned in Article 4. above is granted to him/her by the company *[Company Name]* as settlement of all claims resulting from the termination of his/her contract of employment.

Consequently, and in reciprocity to the payments of the amounts stated in Articles 3 and 4 above, *[Mr or Ms; First and Last Name]'* expressly declares that he/she has no complaints of whatever nature against the company *[Company Name]* or any of its subsidiaries or entities, and that he/she waives all of his/her rights, actions, and claims resulting from the execution or the enforcement of his termination, whether it be in form or substance.

[Mr or Ms; First and Last Name]' declares that he/she is fully informed of his/her status with the Social Security Agencies, Unemployment and the Tax administration. He/she further declares that these issues could not, in any case be used to put the present agreement back in question.

[Mr or Ms; First and Last Name]' pledges himself to withdraw, at his own cost, and before signing this agreement, any action or suit he/she might have brought before any

soit, avant la signature des présentes, du chef de l'exécution et de la rupture de son contrat de travail.

Enfin, en raison du caractère absolument définitif qu'elles entendent donner au présent accord, les parties déclarent expressément qu'il est de leur intention que cet accord constitue une transaction, aux termes des dispositions des articles 2044 et suivants du code civil, de sorte qu'il ne pourra être remis en cause, par l'une ou par l'autre des parties, pour quelque motif que ce soit, et notamment pour erreur de fait ou de droit.

ARTICLE 6

Le présent accord transactionnel a un caractère confidentiel et tant la société *[dénomination]* que *[Monsieur ou Madame, prénom, nom]* s'engagent à ne pas en divulguer le contenu à des tiers, à l'exception toutefois, le cas échéant, des administrations sociale (URSSAF) et fiscale.

Fait à *[ville]*,

Le *[date,*

En double exemplaire.

Pour la société *[dénomination]*

[Monsieur ou Madame, prénom, nom]

Pour l'employé

[Monsieur ou Madame, prénom, nom]

Parapher chaque page et faire précéder la signature de la mention manuscrite *'Lu et approuvé sans réserve ni contrainte - bon pour accord transactionnel définitif et irrévocable et renonciation à toutes instances et actions'*.

court and in any jurisdiction, related to the execution or enforcement of his termination.

Finally, and because of the absolutely final dispositions both parties intend to give to this agreement, both parties expressly agree that this agreement is a transaction as defined in articles 2044 and following of the French Civil Code, so that it may not be put back in question, by either party, for whatever reason, and in particular on the grounds of a miscarriage of facts or of Law.

ARTICLE 6

This agreement is confidential and both the company *[Company Name]* and *[Mr or Ms; First and Last Name]*' pledge themselves not to divulge its contents to third parties with the exception, if so requested, by the Social (URSSAF) or Fiscal authorities.

Signed in *[city]*

On [*date*],

In duplicate copies

For the company [Company Name]

[Mr or Ms; First and Last Name]'

For the employee

[Mr or Ms; First and Last Name]'

Sign each page and have the following handwritten note precede each signature: *"read and approved without reservation nor coercion accepted as such as final and irrevocable compromise agreement and as waiver of all instances and claims"*.

Sample termination agreement: Germany

Between

The Employer

...

...

(Hereafter 'The Employer')

and

[name]
[address]

Hereafter 'The Employee'

A TERMINATION AGREEMENT

is concluded as follows:

Art. 1
Termination date

The existing employment agreement between The Employer and The Employee shall be terminated effective [date], pursuant to the request of The Employer and due to business reasons. The Employee is released irrevocably from her/his duty to work with immediate effect.

Art. 2
Indemnity

The Employer shall, according to Sects. 9 and 10 KSchG (Termination of Employment Act), pay a gross compensation to The Employee in the sense of Sects. 3 No. 9, 24 No. 1, 34 EStG (Income Tax Act) in the amount of € [Amount].

The compensation amount shall be due for payment on [date].

Any applicable taxes and social security contributions shall be borne by The Employee.

The Employee will take her/his holiday claims which are due to her/him until the termination of the employment. The Employer and The Employee have agreed that there are no actual preconditions for further claims or holiday compensation claims and any existing claims have already been compensated for.

Art. 3
Confidentiality and Obligation to Secrecy

The parties to this agreement shall treat the contents of it as strictly confidential and shall not make it accessible to third parties.

The Employee pledges herself/himself to secrecy with regard to any knowledge of business secrets that he/she may have gained through his/her employment.

Art. 4
Obligation to Return

The Employee shall return all documents, keys or other objects owned by The Employer which she/he is in possession of no later than [date], to the department of human resources in [City].

The Employee shall return the company car with the registered licence number [Number] on [date], to the office in [City].

Art. 5
Reference

The Employer shall issue a reference for The Employee which shall contain information regarding type and duration of The Employee's employment, his/her conduct and performance.

Art. 6
Settlement of All Claims

The parties to this agreement have agreed that all mutual claims from the employment contract shall be settled with the execution of this agreement, irrespective of what legal cause they may arise from.

Art. 7
Final Clause

Should any of the provisions of this agreement be invalid, this shall not affect the remaining provisions. Instead of the invalid provision, The Employee and The Employer shall agree upon another valid provision which comes as close as possible to the invalid provision.

Art. 8
Jurisdiction

These terms are to be construed in accordance with and subject to German Law.

place, this [date], _____

The Employer _____

The Employee_____

Sample termination agreement: Italy

Draft: [ ] [date],

MINISTRY OF LABOR AND SOCIAL SECURITY

Provincial Office of Labor of [City]
Provincial Commission for the Settlement of individual controversies

Records of settlement - Index No. ..

On the [day] of [month] at [time] in the Provincial Office of Labor of [City], before the Provincial Commission instituted by Decree No. 255 of January 15, 1974 by the Director of the *U.P.L.M.O* (Provincial Employment Office) of Milan in accordance with Article 410 of the Italian code of civil procedure, composed of:

- Mr/Ms _____, Chairman;
- Mr/Ms _____, Employers' representative;
- Mr/Ms _____, Employees' representative;

the following persons appeared:

- Mr/Ms [Name], resident at [City];
- on behalf of [Company Name], Mr/Ms [Name] vested with representative powers;

for the discussion of the procedure between Mr/Ms [Name] and [Company Name] having the following subject:

TERMINATION OF EMPLOYMENT RELATIONSHIP AND PAYMENT OF AN INCENTIVE TO LEAVE

I. **Preliminary Considerations**

1. on [date], Mr/Ms [Name] was employed by [Company Name] in the capacity of [Title] and with the function of [Function];

2. as a consequence of the changes in [Company Name]'s business strategies Mr/Ms [Name] is available to terminate the employment by mutual consent [**subject to amendments**];

3. the parties, after having discussed the legal and economic aspects of the matter, have agreed to a friendly settlement as follows;

II. **Termination Date**

4. The premises are an integral and substantial part of this agreement.

5. The parties declare that Mr/Ms [Name]'s employment with [Company Name] is terminated by mutual consent effective as of [date], with mutual waiver of the notice period and the indemnity in lieu of such.

III. **Indemnity**

6.   [Company Name] offers to Mr/Ms [Name], who accepts, the gross amount of € [...] as a general settlement pursuant to articles 1965 of the Italian Civil Code and as incentive to leave pursuant Article 12, IV paragraph, letter b) of Law no. 153 of April 30, 1969 and Article 5, Section d), Point 2) of Law 314/1997.

7.   The payment of the amount stated in Article 6. above will be made in full by [Company Name] to Mr/Ms [Name], net of the deductions payable by law, within the term of [...] days from the date of the execution of this agreement together with the severance indemnities accrued as of the date of termination of employment agreement, calculated on the basis of the ordinary salary.

IV. **Return of property**

8.   At the latest on [date], Mr/Ms [Name] will return to [Company representative] or another authorised person all of the documents and property which he received from [Company Name] to perform his/her duties, including but not limited to **[IF APPLICABLE:** the company car, petrol card, portable PC, mobile phone, mobile phone card, credit card, office keys, laptop ...**]** at the registered offices of the Employer.

V. **Claims**

9.   Mr/Ms [Name] acknowledges that [Company Name] has always accurately complied with any obligation, both based on the law, as well as on contract, deriving or connected with the employment agreement, and as much in the relationship between the parties as well as in complying with all the duties to provide notices, to effect payments, or other duties, towards entities or third parties, in any way in connection with the employment relationship.

10. For better clarity Mr/Ms [Name] states and declares that it is his intent to unilaterally and irrevocably waive, in general, all claims against [Company Name], including, but not limited to claims not expressly asserted in relation to his employment and the termination thereof. By way of example, but not limited to the following, Mr/Ms [Name] declares that, regardless of whether it may be against [Company Name] or any other entities of the Group and/or any of their directors, officers and employees, and even in the case where such claims were to happen in the future, his waiver includes the following possible claims:

  • any differences of remuneration or other indemnities;
  • any damages connected with his employment relationship (including intellectual property rights regarding any documents, materials, projects etc. that he/she may have invented, created, etc.);
  • any further reimbursement of expenses or costs borne on behalf of [Company Name];

- any form of compensation in kind, fringe benefits, periodical bonuses, target compensation, incentives;
- any claim concerning withholdings and statutory or contractual contributions on the amounts and benefits in any way paid or that should have been paid by [Company Name], as compensation or for any other reason;
- damages or contributions for any entitlement to a higher level;
- additional pro-rata amounts of monthly installments and any claim concerning indemnity in lieu-of-holidays, or any damages or indemnities based on or connected thereto;
- additional compensation, contributions, indemnities and damages for the performance of overtime work;
- biological damages or damages in any way affecting Mr/Ms [Name]'s overall physical and psychological health;
- any calculation differences of any amounts due by virtue of the law or collective contracts in connection with his employment and/or the termination thereof; including any interest and monetary revaluation on any claim, including but not limited to all of the above.

VI. Secrecy and Confidentiality

11. Mr/Ms [Name] and [Company Name] agree that this Agreement will be treated as a confidential agreement and that they will not disclose any information in this respect, either within or outside of the company of [Company Name], except to persons who must be informed about the content of this Agreement in order to enforce it.

12. Mr/Ms [Name] agrees that he will not make any untrue statement in relation to any Group Company or its offices or staff or make any statement which is intended to or which may have the effect of damaging or lowering the reputation of any Group Company or its officers or staff.

The parties declare that this settlement was reached according to and by effect of Article 1965 of the Italian Civil Code.

Read, confirmed and signed pursuant to the effects under the last paragraph of Article 2113 of the Italian Civil Code.

The Commission therefore declares the controversy settled.

On behalf of [Company Name]   Mr/Ms [Name]
Mr/Ms [Company Representative]

Certification

The Chairman of the Commission, as constituted above, certifies, after having checked the identification, that the signatures of the parties are in their own hand.

The Chairman of the Commission

Sample termination agreement: United Kingdom

COMPROMISE AGREEMENT

(Under sections 203(2) and 203(3) Employment Rights Act 1996 ('ERA 1996'))

DATE: • 2001 •

PARTIES:

(1)   •   ('the Company')

(2)   •   ('the Employee')

I.   **Termination date**

1)   Your employment is terminated with effect from [   ] ('Termination Date').

II. **Indemnity**

2)   As compensation for loss of employment, you will receive a one time indemnity of [   ] as settlement of all claims and provided you comply with the terms and obligations set forth in this agreement.

3)   The first [£ X'000] of the above sum will be paid without deduction of tax. Tax will be deducted from the balance. Any additional tax or national insurance for which the Company has to account in respect of the payment will be borne by you.

4)   Your bonus will be calculated as follows: [   ].

5)   Until [date] the Company will [Payment of Insurance contributions, Health, Life, etc].

6)   The Company agrees to make a contribution of [£X00 plus VAT] towards your personal legal fees in relation to advice as to the terms and effect of this Agreement.

III. **Return of Property**

7)   You undertake to return immediately to the Company all property, equipment, records, keys, credit cards, correspondence, documents, files and other information (whether originals, copies or extracts) belonging to the Company in your possession, custody or control and you confirm that you have not retained any copies.

IV. **Claims**

8)   You confirm that you have no claims against the Company [or any of its subsidiaries] in any jurisdiction whether at common law, under

contract, or Statute, or pursuant to European Community law including, without limitation, any claim which you may have against the Company [or any of its subsidiaries], its officers or employees arising directly or indirectly from your employment or office or its termination, including, without limitation, any claim relating to [wrongful dismissal], [remuneration or expenses], [breach of the Working Time Regulations 1998], [unfair dismissal], [redundancy], [equal pay], [sex discrimination], [race discrimination], Part II of ERA 1996, Part II of Disability Discrimination Act 1995 ('DDA 1995') or any other claim which might be made by you to a court or tribunal.

9)   The Company acknowledges that it has no claim against you arising out of your employment or any other matter whatsoever. The Company agrees not to institute any proceedings against you before an Employment Tribunal.

V.   Statements, Secrecy & Confidentiality

10)   You will not make any untrue statement in relation to any Group Company or its offices or staff or make any statement which is intended to or which may have the effect of damaging or lowering the reputation of any Group Company or its officers or staff.

11)   The terms of this letter and all discussions and other correspondence on this subject shall be treated by you as confidential and you will not disclose them to any other person except as may be required by law or regulatory authorities or with the Company's written consent.

12)   The Company and you agree that the conditions regulating compromise agreements under section 203(3) ERA 1996, [section 77(4A) Sex Discrimination Act 1975, section 72(4A) Race Relations Act 1976 and section 9(3) DDA 1995] have been satisfied.

VI.   Date of payment

13)   Payment of all sums [and receipt of the benefits referred to above] will be made within seven days of the [later of] receipt by the Company of your signed acceptance of these terms [and the director resignation letters referred in [   ] below] [and the Termination Date].

14)   You confirm that the payment is in full and final settlement of your claim against the Company for [**state nature of claim**].

VII.   Execution

15)   On execution of this agreement, the agreement will be considered to be an open document and able to be submitted as evidence of a binding agreement in any court of law.

16) [Within 2 days of execution of this agreement, you agree to write to the tribunal withdrawing any claims which you may have and payment will not be made until acceptable evidence has been presented to the Company that such a notification had been made to the tribunal.]

17) You represent and warrant that:

a. you have received independent legal advice from [identify adviser], a qualified lawyer, as to the terms and effect of this Agreement prior to signing it, and in particular its effect on your ability to pursue your rights before an Employment Tribunal and that on the basis of that advice, you accept the terms of this agreement;

b. you are advised by the qualified lawyer that there is in force and was, at the time that you received the advice referred to above, a policy of insurance covering the risk of a claim by you in respect of loss arising in consequence of that advice.

VIII. **Jurisdiction**

18) These terms are to be construed in accordance with and subject to English law.

Signed by
for and on behalf of
the Company
in the presence of:

Signed by
for and on behalf of
the Employee
in the presence of:

Sample termination agreement: Switzerland

Employee Name
Address
Zip & City

Registered Mail with acknowledgment of receipt

PRIVATE & CONFIDENTIAL

DATE

Dear [Employee Name],

Further to the recent company announcement, and your individual discussions with [Supervisor/MD], I regret to confirm to you that for economic reasons the [Company Name] operation is to be significantly reduced.

After careful consideration, we have not found any alternative employment for you either in (Switzerland) or any other [Company Name] location.

As a result, I am writing to confirm formally that your employment will terminate by reason of redundancy with effect on DATE ('the Termination Date') and in accordance with the terms stated in your contract and the Swiss Code of Obligations.

SALARY & COMPENSATION

You will be paid salary [and any outstanding commissions/bonus [in full/pro-rata or as follows]] to the Termination Date, together with any accrued but untaken holiday.

[Note: optional] In accordance with your contract of employment, you will not be required to work the period of your notice, and the Company will make a payment in lieu of your notice for this period (less tax and Social contributions).

[Note: optional] In addition, the Company will also make a further payment to you as a token of goodwill and thanks for your contribution (Company Redundancy Payment).

The payments you will receive are as follows:

Notice period   : According to Swiss Law (or employment contract)
                               [specify number of months]
Bonus   : 100% equivalent to x month salaries
Redundancy payment : (optional)
Holidays in Lieu   : *[specify number of days]*

Salary will be computed on the basis of base salary plus forfeit expenses as stated in your contract. Payments will be made via payroll in the usual way, no later than

[date], (normally the last contractual date of employment which will be 1 or 2 months following notification, but may be earlier).

May we also draw to your attention that as of (DATE), you will no longer be insured against health and accident hazards and that you will need to take out personal insurance to that effect.

OBLIGATIONS

You are reminded of your obligations to the Company in terms of confidentiality and disclosure of information. Please ensure that you return any and all items of company property and information before the end of [date].

These terms are in full and final settlement of all matters arising out of your employment with [Company Name].

The Company very much regrets this situation, which is a business decision and no reflection on your role or performance. Please contact either Supervisor or myself if you have any questions.

We wish you the best of luck in your future career.

Yours sincerely

[Company representative]

Additional provisions which may be necessary (all countries)

1. The Company will maintain private medical insurance on the same terms on which you [and your family] currently enjoy these benefits until [   ]/for a period of [   ] from the Termination Date or until the date on which you take up full time employment with another employer whichever is sooner.

2. You will be entitled to retain your company car, registration number [   ] [for your own personal use only] for a period of [   ] from the Termination Date or until the date upon which you take up full time employment with another employer, whichever is sooner, during which time:

    a. the Company will pay all running costs in respect of the car other than the cost of petrol and motor oil;

    b. you will keep the car in good and roadworthy condition;

    c. you will not do anything whereby any insurance policy effected by the Company in respect of the car is vitiated or avoided; [add any other condition imposed by insurer] and

    d. you will at all times comply with the Company's car policy.

    e. You will return the car together with the keys to the Company's premises at [   ] on or before [   ] 20[   ].

3. You acknowledge that your option(s) under the [   ] Share Option Scheme lapse on [the Termination Date]/may be exercised subject to the rules of the scheme at any time from [the Termination Date] in [   ] [on the basis that you were made redundant on the Termination Date].

4. You will sign the enclosed stock transfer forms transferring shares held by you as a nominee for the Company and you will transfer all other shares held by you in trust or as a nominee by virtue of your employment with the Company to such persons as the Company may direct.

5. You will sign the enclosed letters of resignation as a director of each Group Company and you will forthwith resign all other directorships or offices [(including trusteeship of the Company's pension scheme)] which you hold by virtue of your employment with the Company.

    a. ['Group Company' means any one of the Company, its subsidiaries, its holding company or any subsidiary of its holding company (in each case as defined by section 736 of the Companies Act 1985) and 'the Group' has the corresponding meaning.]

6. Having resigned as a director of the Company and from such other offices as you hold within the Group you will not conduct yourself in any way

inconsistent with having surrendered your authority either in matters of internal company administration or externally, and following the termination of your employment, you will not represent yourself as being a director of, or employed by, or connected in any way with any Group Company.

7. You will provide the Company with such assistance as it may require in the conduct of proceedings in the High Court of Justice Action Number [   ] brought by/against [   ] and such other proceedings as may arise in respect of which the Company or its legal advisors believes you may be able to provide assistance and the Company will pay your reasonable expenses incurred in providing such assistance insofar as your assistance cannot be compelled or by a court of competent jurisdiction.

8. You will not without the consent in writing of the Company divulge to any person or use for your own benefit or the benefit of any person any information of private, secret or confidential nature concerning the business, accounts or finances of any Group Company or any of the secrets, dealings, transactions or affairs of any Group Company or of any customer or client of any Group Company which have come to your knowledge during the course of your employment with a Group Company [or previously or otherwise].

9. You will not for a period of [   ] from the Termination Date directly or indirectly be interested or concerned (whether as shareholder, director, employee, sub-contractor, partner, consultant, proprietor, agent or otherwise) in any business within a radius of [   ] miles of [   ] competing with any business carried on at the Termination Date by any Group Company with which you were actively concerned at any time within one year preceding the Termination Date. However this restriction does not prevent you from being the holder or beneficial owner (for investment purposes only) of any class of securities in any company if such class of securities is listed or dealt in on any recognised investment exchange and you (together with your spouse, children, parents and parents' issue) neither hold nor are beneficially interested in more than five per cent of any single class of the securities in that company.

10. You will not without the consent in writing of the Company for a period of [   ] from the Termination Date (either personally or by your agent or by letters, circulars or advertisements and whether for yourself or on behalf of any other person) canvass or solicit orders (for services similar to those being provided by any Group Company at the Termination Date and with which you were actively concerned at any time within one year preceding the Termination Date from any person who is at the Termination Date or has been at any time within one year before the Termination Date been a customer of any Group Company with which you have been actively concerned at any time within one year before the Termination Date.

11.   You will not for a period of [   ] from the Termination Date directly or indirectly employ any employee of a Group Company or (either personally or by your agent and whether for yourself or on behalf of any other person) offer employment to or induce or encourage any employee of a Group Company to leave its employment.

HR Due Diligence checklist

	Compared with acquiring company	Potential liabilities		Potential costs involved
		Compliance checked		
General compensation items				
Salaries of management				
Salaries of employees				
Commission systems				
Profit participation schemes				
Bonus and financial commitments				
Contractual termination agreement				
Non-competition clauses				
Special retirement plans				
Stock option plans				
Tax effective compensation systems				
Benefits				
Holidays				
Sick/Maternity leave				
Sabbatical leaves				
Training commitments				
Pension plan				
Health/Accident insurance				
Life insurance				
Company cars				
Lunch facilities				
Clubs and entertainment				
Other benefits				
HR systems				
HR MIS systems and compatibility				
Cost of maintenance				
Accuracy and availability of data				
Manpower needed for maintenance				
Statistical data				
Turnover				
Absenteeism				
On/Off site accidents				
Overtime				
Women in management				
Age groups (and pre-retirement issues)				
Educational level				

Integration plan

Item	Action	Responsible manager	To be actioned by	Deadline	Progress report
Steps to the integration plan	1. Setting up the plan 2. Prepare the communication plan 3. Compare terms of employment 4. Compare benefits 5. Compare systems and policies 6. Emergency measures: Prepare retention programmes 7. Review global processes 8. Conduct manpower planning, assessments and redundancies 9. Finalize transfers and integration				
1. Setting up the plan	Assign responsibilities and empower leaders Define integration team organization Define the basis and timelines for reporting				
2. Prepare the communication plan	Empower the communication team leader Agree HR communication milestones and key stakeholders Define communication tools Develop questions and answers and communication guidelines				
3. Compare terms of employment	Analyse differences in contractual terms of employment Review the employment contracts Analyse salary and commission systems				
4. Compare benefits	Compare medical coverage Compare old age and retirement benefits Compare life insurances Social and other benefits				
5. Compare systems and policies	HRMIS systems, tools and date transfer Compare general policies and handbooks				
6. Prepare retention programmes	Programmes to retain key players during the integration process Programmes to retain employees throughout the process				
7. Review global processes	Review products and sales Review vocabulary used for job description and responsibilities				
8. Conduct manpower planning, assessments and redundancies	Define manpower needs Conduct assessments and skill reviews Define redundancy strategy and guidelines Establish termination and severance package guidelines Implement helpdesks and hotlines				
9. Finalize transfers and integration	Announce transfers, appointments and new reporting lines Integrate new employees Provide coaching, follow up and feedback				

Sample reporting form

Pre-reporting form

Team		Team leader					
Date		Phone number					
Country	Key issues	Potential risk/liability		Urgency	Next step	By (date)	Status
General comments:							

Examples of topics and media support

Issue	*Media*	Event	General meeting	Restricted meeting	One-on-one meeting	Video conference	Telephone conference	Update	Regular newsletter	Personal letter	Flyer	Intranet	e-mail	How-to tool kit	Other
Major announcement															
General announcements															
Select audience announcements															
CEO updates															
HR updates															
New appointments															
Resignations															
Structural changes															
Communication guidelines															
Transitional policies															
Policy changes															
HR general issues															
Redundancy/Downsizing															
Q&A															
Helpdesk support															
Other stakeholder communications															
Other															

Salary practice analysis

	Company A	Company B	Minimum legal requirement	Plan
Base salary				
Management				
Sales staff				
Support staff				
Salary instalments				
Pay date				
Pay mode				
Commission				
Sales staff				
Individual performance bonus				
Sales functions				
Support function				

Salary practice analysis (continued)

	Company A	Company B	Minimum legal requirement	Plan
Profit sharing				
Management				
Staff				
Overtime policy				
Management				
Staff				
Salary review policy				
Management				
Staff				
Special payments				
Expenses for relevant staff				

Comparative analysis of life insurance

Coverage	Plan A	Plan B	Comments
Base coverage			
Maximum coverage			
Capitalization			
Eligibility and duration			
Life insurance of spouse and dependants			
Contributions			

Comparative benefits analysis

Benefit	Legal requirements	Company A	Company B	Comment
Holidays				
Working week				
Retirement age				
Overtime				
Profit sharing				
Stock option plan				
Expense policy				

Comparative benefits analysis (continued)

Benefit	Legal requirements	Company A	Company B	Comment
Travel policy				
Company car				
Luncheon vouchers				
Clubs and facilities				
Other				

Comparative benefits process analysis

Benefit	Request document	Deadlines	Process	Comment
Holidays				
Illness Accident				
Retirement				
Overtime				
Profit sharing				
Stock option plan				

Comparative benefits process analysis (continued)

Benefit	Request document	Deadlines	Process	Comment
Expense policy				
Travel policy				
Company car				
Lunch vouchers				
Clubs and facilities				
Other	A			

Note: A refers to Company A. B refers to Company B

Example of a criteria matrix for weighting candidates

	a) Impact of errors will be limited to work and will have no, or hardly any effect on the course of business	b) Impact of errors may create delays or costs but without seriously affecting the course of business	c) Errors may cause serious delays, extra costs, and loss of revenue or client dissatis- faction, which will have a direct impact on reputation, production or profits	d) Errors could seriously damage the company's reputation, productivity, treasury, and overall revenues; or create serious liabilities
1. Executes work given by superior				
2. Does mainly execution work but may decide on minor changes or timings				
3. Does some execution work, but takes own decisions in the execution process. Has limited delegation authority				
4. Works autonomously on the basis of specific guidelines. May delegate simple execution work				
5. Works autonomously on the basis of general guidelines. May delegate execution work				
6. Ensures some complex tasks, involving several parameters and requiring autonomy and initiative				
7. Ensures complex tasks requiring superior skills, knowledge and management abilities				
8. Ensures very complex tasks requiring superior skills, vision, and strategic ability				

Basic assessment of the position (manages 12 area sales directors)

Key criteria	Grade range requirement				W
Business development					
Business acumen	1–10				
Strategic thinking	1–10				
P&L Management	1–10				
Presentation skills	1–10				
Technical skills	1–10				
Management					
Leadership ability	1–5				
Decision making	1–5				
Writing/Communication skills	1–5				
Problem solving	1–5				
Integrity	1–5				
Personal					
Intellectual aptitude	1–3				
Creativity	1–3				
Willingness to travel	1–3				
Willingness to relocate	1–3				
Language skills	1–3				
Score					

	Below average	Average	Above average
Business Development	1–6	7–8	9–10
Management	1–3	4	5
Personal	1	2	3

Index